Why
Johnny *Still*
Can't Read

Ex Libris

Dorothy E. Moffitt

Why Johnny *Still* Can't Read

A New Look at the Scandal of Our Schools

Rudolf Flesch

author of *Why Johnny Can't Read*

Foreword by Mary L. Burkhardt

HARPER COLOPHON BOOKS

HARPER & ROW, PUBLISHERS

NEW YORK, CAMBRIDGE, PHILADELPHIA, SAN FRANCISCO

LONDON, MEXICO CITY, SAO PAULO, SYDNEY

A hardcover edition of this book is published by Harper & Row, Publishers, Inc.

A portion of this work originally appeared in *Family Circle*.

First Harper Colophon edition published 1983.

Designer: C. Linda Dingler

Library of Congress Cataloging in Publication Data

Flesch, Rudolf Franz, 1911-
  Why Johnny still can't read: A new look at the scandal of our schools.
  Bibliography: p.
  Includes index.
  1. Reading (Elementary)—Phonetic method. I. Title.
LB1573.F552 1981   372.4'145   80-8686
ISBN 0-06-091031-3 (pbk.)

---

85 86 87 10 9 8 7 6 5 4

To my family,
who had to put up with me during
"the year of the book"

Contents

Acknowledgments

My first great debt of gratitude is to Mrs. Kathryn Diehl of Lima, Ohio, former research director of the Reading Reform Foundation. She put her enormous knowledge of the field and vast stores of material totally at my disposal and helped me in innumerable ways. I am immensely grateful to her.

Second, I am obliged to the Reading Reform Foundation of Scottsdale, Arizona, and its dynamic president, Mrs. Bettina Rubicam. Both have committed themselves to this project wholeheartedly and furnished me with masses of materials and information. Again, I am immensely grateful.

Third, my thanks go to Mr. John V. Gordon of Redgranite, Wisconsin, who is a walking encyclopedia—and delightfully outspoken—on this subject. He has sent me vast amounts of material and has been consistently encouraging. Thanks a lot!

Now comes a list of organizations and persons who helped me with free material or opened their doors to my visits:

American Montessori Society, and Ms. Judith Delman, New York City.

Children's Television Workshop, New York City, and Dr. Edward Palmer.

Educators Publishing Service, Cambridge, Massachusetts, and Ms. Elaine Bayer.

Family Circle magazine, New York City, which permitted me to reprint an article published in its pages as my first chapter.

The Fortune Society, New York City, and Mrs. Margaret Bishop.

Kurzweil Computer Products, Cambridge, Massachusetts, and its president Raymond Kurzweil.

Mount Vernon Public Schools, Mount Vernon, New York, and Mrs. Ruth Cafarella.

Charles E. Merrill Publishing Co., Columbus, Ohio.

Open Court Publishing Co., LaSalle, Illinois, and its president M. Blouke Carus.

P.S. 30, Jamaica, Queens, New York City, and its principal Mrs. Ursula Day.

P.S. 251, Brooklyn, New York, and its principal Mrs. Cynthia Kamen.

The following persons have all been most helpful and obliging and gave me valuable material or advice:

Dr. Richard L. Allington, Albany, N.Y.
Dr. Barbara L. Bateman, Eugene, Ore.
Mr. Samuel Blumenfeld, Boston, Mass.
Mrs. Mary L. Burkhardt, Rochester, N.Y., who wrote the foreword.
Dr. Douglas Carnine, Eugene, Ore.
Dr. Carol Chomsky, Cambridge, Mass.
Miss Ann M. Doyle, West Palm Beach, Fla.
Mr. Siegfried Engelmann, Eugene, Ore.
Dr. Dina Feitelson, Jerusalem, Israel
Dr. Robert M. Gagné, Tallahassee, Fla.
Dr. Philip B. Gough, Austin, Tex.
Dr. Patrick Groff, San Diego, Calif.
Dr. Mary R. Hoover, Jacksonville, Fla.
Mrs. Mary Johnson, Winnipeg, Man., Canada
Dr. E. I. Juliet, Ardsley, N.Y.
Mrs. Hedy Levenback, New York City
Mrs. Margaret McEathron, Seal Beach, Calif.
Dr. Linda A. Meyer, Urbana-Champaign, Ill.
Dr. Hilde Mosse, New York City
Mrs. Jean Osborn, Urbana-Champaign, Ill.
Dr. Cecelia Pollack, Great Neck, N.Y.
Miss Geraldine Rodgers, Lyndhurst, N.J.
Dr. S. Jay Samuels, Minneapolis, Minn.
Dr. Robert L. Thorndike, New York City
Dr. Richard L. Venezky, Newark, Del.
Dr. Charles C. Walcutt, Great Neck, N.Y.
Dr. Joanna Williams, New York City
Mr. Kenneth L. Woodward, Briarcliff Manor, N.Y.

I also want to express my extreme gratitude for the ever-ready help and advice of the staff of Mercy College Library, Dobbs Ferry, New York, which hospitably opened its doors to me.

Finally, I want to thank my two splendid typists, Mrs. Barbara Koenig and Mr. Bert M. Joel. Their expert help was wholly indispensable.

RUDOLF FLESCH

Dobbs Ferry, N.Y.
July 1980

Foreword

Since I was already "taught" to be a reading failure by the time Dr. Flesch wrote *Why Johnny Can't Read* in 1955, I think that I am especially suited to write the foreword to his second book on the subject, written twenty-five years later. Unfortunately, I not only know about the reading problem in our schools, but I am well aware of how it feels to be labeled a reading failure. Feeling is a lot more acute than just knowing! Needless to say, when Dr. Flesch asked if I would be willing to write the foreword, my response was an enthusiastic "Yes!" In doing so, I hope my professional experiences will support Dr. Flesch's findings, and at the same time have an important message for you and your children.

First, I would like to share with you a few personal experiences and the hope that your children never have to suffer as I did in school. The year 1947 found me in North Carolina where I entered kindergarten and learned to play and socialize better than I had. Reading was not allowed. The next year I was placed in a look-say reading program. Entering first grade was going to be such fun because I would finally learn to read.

All too soon the reality was that reading was nothing more than a difficult guessing game. The teacher would show me a picture of a dog and then the word *dog*. The next day when the teacher asked me to read, I would read *dog* for the word *did*. In front of the class I would be stopped by the teacher and told that I missed a word. Throughout my first-grade year, I repeatedly had this type of negative experience.

Whenever I was at home and tried to read one of my books, my interest was killed because I could not read many of the words. My grandmother would tell me just to sound out the words! I did not know what she meant because I was being taught to read by looking at a picture and then trying to remember the word that matched. In desperation she asked my teacher if she could teach me to sound out words, but was told that this would only confuse me, and in the long run hurt my ability to read.

Several years later (even though my family was afraid to help me) my grandmother decided that enough guessing and stumbling on words was enough. Night after night, she sat me down and taught me how to sound out words. I will never forget how she could sound out a word she had never seen before. Once she pronounced the word, she would say, "Oh, I have heard of that word," and then tell me what it meant. The nightmare was over. I understood the mystery of words and reading was easy. From that day on, none of the teachers talked about the possibility of my repeating a grade. I was a successful reader, visited the library several times a week, and read books, books, books. However, there was still one problem in school: The stories in my look-say readers were dull and boring; but that's another problem I will address later.

By the time I entered college, I had decided that I wanted to teach reading in a large city school district. Furthermore, I wanted to make sure that all the children I taught would easily and quickly learn to read. Since I was an only child, books had become close friends and an endless joy in my life.

Most of my professional career has been spent as a reading teacher, Title I Reading Supervisor, and Director of Reading (Kindergarten through Grade 12) in the City School District of Rochester, New York. When I entered the district in 1966, the student population was 40,000 (40 percent minority). Now it is 35,000 (57 percent minority). I am sure that you have often heard it said that the percentage of children who are minority influences the degree of reading failure in a given school or district. Reality is that whether children are "advantaged" or "disadvantaged," black or white, rich or poor, does not have anything to do with how successfully children learn to read. Based on my professional experiences, such statements are only excuses for not teaching children to read.

My first teaching assignment in Rochester was as a teacher of reading, English, and history in a large inner-city high school, grades 7, 8, and 11. Many of my students had previously been told that maybe reading just wasn't their thing, that they should just keep working and try not to worry about their reading problem. I tested each of my students with a diagnostic reading test and the results were that most of them had a decoding problem. They were expending a great deal of time and energy guessing at words rather than being able to sound them out. Another frustration was that they spent so much of their energy struggling with the unknown words that the meaning of the passage was lost. When this happens, you can observe the child reading in a hesitant manner and often even mumbling the words. The child is not able to read fluently, confidently decoding the more difficult words, reading complete phrases and thus reading for meaning. Reading could and would be my students' "thing to do," and by the end of each year their reading performance improved tremendously.

After my second year of teaching in a junior-senior high school, I wanted to teach at the elementary level and discover how so many children were getting to high school with so few reading skills. Fortunately, my next assignment was as a Title I remedial reading teacher in an inner-city elementary school with a population of more than one thousand Kindergarten through Grade 7 students. I spent four challenging years working daily with children who needed remedial reading instruction. Again and again, the problem was that even sixth graders were still guessing at words

I learned so much in those four years that it is hard to summarize my findings briefly. First, I'll point out two important observations: (1) my students were alert and anxious to learn, and (2) the teaching staff was extremely dedicated and worked long, hard hours. At that time, only look-say and eclectic programs (not phonics-first) were used in the school. These types of programs were also in use in all of the other 45 elementary schools. In spite of the teachers' hard work and the childrens' readiness and willingness to learn, children were having trouble learning to read. In fact, remedial readers were being generated in my school faster than I could remediate them.

My experience as a Title I Elementary Reading Teacher raised some crucial questions in my mind. Why should children receive one reading program in the classroom, and then have to go out of the classroom to receive remedial instruction in phonics? Why not teach reading so that children learn successfully the first time they are taught?

I will never forget little Michael. He was a fifth grader with a smile and eagerness to learn. Michael came to me each day, along with nine other students, for remedial instruction. Since the students were still having trouble decoding, I spent part of each day's half-hour lesson developing phonics skills.

Michael said something during one of our remedial sessions that should be a lesson to us all. One of the words in the story we were reading was *astronaut*. To make my students use the phonics skills I taught them, I did not pronounce words for them but, instead, had them apply their skills by sounding out the unknown words. When I asked one of the other students in Michael's group to sound out *astronaut*, he slowly but surely did so. Just as he pronounced the word, I heard Michael say, "So that's what the word *astronaut* looks like!" The word had probably been in Michael's listening and speaking vocabulary for a long time. Perhaps he understood and could say *astronaut* before he ever came to school.

Obviously, the lesson for us is that children come to school with a tremendously rich listening and speaking vocabulary. As soon as they are able to sound out words, they can enter them into their reading and spelling vocabulary. Once they can decode a word, they then may automatically know the meaning. If the word read is totally new to the child, he can then immediately be taught its meaning.

I moved on to become the Title I Reading Supervisor for Elementary and Secondary Reading Programs. Those were fast and furious years. The Title I Reading Teachers worked with me to remediate students as rapidly and successfully as possible. Title I students daily received an extra "shot" of reading instruction. The reading teachers worked to teach them the phonics and comprehension skills they needed. Each student was tested throughout the entire school year. The teacher was teaching-testing; teaching-testing; and individualizing instruction to meet each student's reading needs. After three years, the proof was again evident. Students who were thought of as having limited reading capabilities made significant progress every year. Again it was clear that reading is not a mysterious act. The Title I remedial assistance was providing children the instruction they should have received in their regular classroom reading program. When taught logically and systematically, reading becomes a natural accomplishment for the child. If we could only recognize and appreciate the very logical auditory and visual process the child goes through when learning to read, we could save ourselves from all the reading "fads," "bandwagons," and "shortcuts" that add to the great confusion about how children learn to read.

Now the year was 1974 and the Title I remedial programs were accelerating the students more rapidly than the regular look-say or eclectic programs. The Board of Education took a stand. Students' reading performance in Rochester, New York, was to improve. By the end of grade one, students' average reading performance was already three months below grade level as measured on standardized tests. Sixth graders were almost twenty months (two full school years) below grade level. Reading instruction was in trouble and students were the losers.

Finally, there would be a Reading Department K–12 with a reading teacher/trainer in each school and a districtwide Director of Reading to be responsible for providing a local reading program that would teach children to read. To this day, I have been thankful that I was the person chosen to serve as Director of Reading. Every moment has been filled with challenge and reward. I will try to explain the process the Rochester City School District engaged in, since its educators have been seriously committed to teaching all children to read.

During the first year in my new position, I frequently visited the 46 elementary schools. My visits revealed that kindergartners were not being challenged in a formal reading readiness program; students received a minimum of phonics instruction (only what was provided in non-phonics-first programs); entirely different programs were being used at various grade levels within the same school; the time allocation for reading instruction was often disturbed by numerous interruptions; there was little or no day-to-day measurement of students' reading skills and progress; and finally there were frustrated students, teachers, and parents.

Based on these observations, it appeared to me that students' reading difficulties were not of their own making and could be solved by improving the reading instructional program within the schools. It was time to stop asking, "What's wrong with Johnny?" It was time to ask ourselves, "What must we do to teach Johnny to read?"

The following school year a committee of forty members was asked to join me in a comprehensive study to end reading failure in the Rochester City School District. It included parents, community group representatives, teachers, and administrators. Letters were sent to over fifty publishers to submit their reading programs for our consideration and study.

After an exhaustive study, the committee members voted unanimously to select what they judged to be the three best programs on the market: Lippincott, now published by Harper & Row; Open Court Correlated Language Arts Program, published by Open Court; and Distar, published by Science Research Associates. This recommendation was approved by the Board of Education, and the newly adopted programs were placed at the kindergarten through third grade levels in the 1976–77 school year and in grades four through six in 1977–78. The cost of the materials was $250,000 per year. Thus, a commitment to improved reading instruction had been taken by a district and its Board.

All teachers and school administrators received extensive inservice training in the proper delivery and supervision of the programs before they were implemented in the schools. Even the best programs will fail if they are not delivered by well-prepared teachers and monitored by well-informed administrators. Too often, teachers are expected to deliver new programs with little or no training.

Each school faculty was asked to select the reading program to be used with their students. They had the option of selecting: Lippincott (Kindergarten–6); Open Court (Kindergarten–6); Distar and Lippincott (3–6); or Distar (Kindergarten–2) and Open Court (3–6). Six of the elementary schools now use Distar, grades K–2, followed by Lippincott or Open Court, grades 3–6. Of the remaining schools, approximately one half use Lippincott in grades K–6 and the other half use Open Court in grades K–6.

Even though the committee's decision was unanimous, you should not think the change to using only three reading programs (and phonics-first programs at that) was an easy one. Previously, there were seven look-say or eclectic reading programs approved for use with students.

More than once I was told that, in a big city, to think of students' reaching grade-level standards was not realistic. Furthermore, if we didn't provide for students' reading needs through many different reading programs, the scores would go down rather than up. During the summer between the time the new reading programs were adopted and implemented, I remember one teacher, who had worked in Rochester for twenty years, stopping me several times in the local drugstore and supermarket to say that we were making a big mistake. Her concern was that many children could not learn phonetically and this would cause reading performance to decline.

My explanation to that veteran teacher was that if we were determined to improve student performance, we must stop asking what was wrong with our students and judging what they can't do and learn. Instead, we must have the courage to organize for change: first, by believing that all children can and will learn to read; second, by taking an educational stand through selecting the best teaching tools (programs) for teacher and student use (even if it means incurring initial criticism); third, by sticking with the task of using programs for a length of time, since the substantial correction of a problem does not happen overnight; and finally, everyone involved in educating the child must work extremely hard. The alternative to that position is dismal and unacceptable. Children continue not to read well and suffer the consequences for the rest of their lives.

The three phonics-first programs were implemented and we all lived through the first months of teaching only one program and a new phonics-first program at that. As usual, change came hard. That Christmas Eve found me rushing out of the post office, when I came face to face with the veteran teacher I spoke of earlier. Her first words were, "Mrs. Burkhardt, I just have one thing to tell you." I took a deep breath and expected the worst. Instead, she said, "I have taught reading in this district for twenty years, but my first graders have never been as far advanced as my students are this year. I just *thought* I was teaching reading before!" Had I really heard what I thought I heard? As we continued to talk, she told me all the reasons a good teacher's teaching is enhanced by a phonics-first program. At that moment, I knew that every day Rochester's students were receiving a special present from their teachers. That gift was effective reading instruction.

Five years later, Rochester's students are readers. Our students' average reading performance is above grade level at grade one and at grade level in grades 2 through 6 as measured by the Metropolitan Reading Achievement Test. Please note that this test measures reading comprehension. This is a dramatic change from only five years ago when one of the major topics of conversation was the number of non-readers in our schools. Today, students automatically decode logically, systematically, and successfully. This enables them to use their energy to read for meaning and understanding, which of course is the ultimate purpose and joy of reading.

I am convinced, without a doubt, that a superior program taught by well-trained teachers enables *all* children to learn to read. In other words, when the better programs are used by teachers, fewer children fall behind in reading performance. Instead, all students are better able to progress and achieve rather than stumbling, guessing, and meeting with less and less reading success. The child who is truly reading disabled (dyslexic) is very rare. When children are taught to read in a structured, teacher-directed instructional program, they read. When this is not done, many children experience difficulty and are then mislabeled as dyslexic, an excuse. Throughout this country, our teachers desperately need to take the best reading programs into the classroom with them. Then they will be able to eliminate the mystery of reading and ensure that children become independent readers. Distinguished researchers, as cited by Dr. Flesch, have completed numerous research studies that document exactly what Rochester's students have demonstrated. One program is *not* as good as another. Instead, phonics-first programs that are logical and responsibly developed make a significant positive difference. One major difference is independent readers who read by Christmas of their first-grade year rather than remaining dependent on instructional programs that delay decoding and thus treat it as a secret to be kept from students. We must not underestimate our children. If the standards are high, children will achieve.

An elementary school librarian recently made a point of

stopping to tell me that second graders come into the library and ask for "chapter books" by well-known authors. Young students also come into the library to find materials on certain topics they research throughout the school year as they develop their "Experts Journal" which is a part of the Open Court Correlated Language Arts Program. Her parting comment was, "Our second-grade students are now reading like our fifth graders used to read. When a child comes into our school, teachers can immediately tell if the student is entering the school from outside the district. Students coming into our district can't read nearly as well as our city children."

Rochester's teachers and students have also clearly shown the positive results that can be realized with junior and senior high students that were reading below grade level. All grade 7–12 students who read below grade level receive daily reading instruction in Open Court Reading Program materials. Once our high school students (these are students who are new to our school or did not have the benefit of phonics-first programs starting in Kindergarten or first grade) are taught to improve their decoding skills and are exposed to quality literature, they too rapidly improve. In fact, some of our students' greatest reading gains have been at the high school level. Never let it be said that if students have not learned to read by the time they are in high school, they will never learn. While it is more difficult to correct a reading problem that has existed for so long, such students should not be considered to be poor readers for years to come. Exceptional instruction and programs can correct almost all reading disabilities. After observing student after student, I know that children and young adults who are taught in synthetic phonics-first programs are then able to read "real" writing rather than writing that is only written at a certain grade level for basal readers. The beauty of the written language is usually lost in graded stories which are in look-say or eclectic programs. Thus, the stories are often repetitious and boring. As reading becomes a successful experience in phonics-first programs, children enjoy reading and it becomes a habit. The reading habit is the best insurance that your child will improve his or her comprehension and critical thinking skills. Also, well-written literature serves as the child's model when writing.

Each week for the last couple of years, I have received one to three calls from educators in other school districts (such as New York City and Cincinnati) who have heard about the reading phenomenon in Rochester, New York. Most of those interested callers have then visited our schools to see for themselves what is taking place. What do they see? Our visitors are delighted to see eager, confident children who are being taught the very logical and simple process of learning to read exceptional classical and contemporary literature. The determination and excitement in the faces of the teachers and students is both encouraging and inspiring.

Dr. Flesch has thoroughly documented his findings. His book should be considered a message of logic and great hope to America's parents, children, and teachers. Through his careful attention to the research literature, the great confusion regarding effective reading instruction could be ended. Reading has become big business in our schools. It is a business that will succeed if the children are not allowed to fail. My special thanks to the courageous Board of Education members, administrators, principals, teachers, students, and parents who have worked with me. The success rate that was thought by some to be the impossible is clearly within our reach. Educators can make the crucial difference for today's children. In Rochester, we have labored to make sure that all children are winners.

You are your child's greatest protection. Any teacher who has ever taught children using a phonics-first program can explain the reasons for the high success rate to you. Like Rochester's students, make sure your children are among the winners. They are just waiting to be taught!

MARY L. BURKHARDT
Director, Department of Reading K–12
City School District, Rochester, N.Y.

Why
Johnny *Still*
Can't Read

1

Why Johnny *Still* Can't Read

Are you worrying about your child's education? You should be. There's an 85 percent chance that your Johnny or Mary will never learn to read properly.

There are two schools of thought about how to teach a child to read. One is called "intensive phonics" or "systematic phonics" or, more recently, "decoding" or "code emphasis." In this book, to avoid confusion, I'll call it "phonics-first." The other is called the "look-and-say" or "whole-word" or "sight-reading" method or—so help me—"psycholinguistics." I'll use "look-and-say."

When I wrote my book *Why Johnny Can't Read** twenty-five years ago, look-and-say ruled supreme. Almost all American schools used it. Phonics-first was a poor orphan, used only in a handful of schools.

I said in my book that phonics-first worked splendidly and should be used in all schools, while look-and-say was wretchedly poor and should be abandoned at once.

Unfortunately my advice fell on deaf ears. With heart-breaking slowness, phonics-first crept into some 15 percent of our schools, but an estimated 85 percent of them still stick to old, discredited look-and-say.

The results of this mass miseducation have been disastrous. America is rapidly sinking into a morass of ignorance. The official statistics are appalling.

In 1975 the U.S. Office of Education sponsored the so-called APL (Adult Performance Level) study, conducted by Dr.

---

* Bibliographical information on references will be found by chapter at the end of the text, starting at page 171.

Norvel Northcutt of the University of Texas in Austin. It was designed to find out how many Americans had the skills to cope with modern life. It showed that 21.7 percent of adults between eighteen and sixty-five—or 23 million people—couldn't read a want ad, a job application form, a label on a medicine bottle, or a safety sign at a workplace.

Of those 23 million, 16 percent had never gone beyond third grade. This left 19 million who'd had four or more years of schooling but never learned how to read. Why? Because almost all of them were taught by look-and-say, and the method doesn't work.

And what happened at the other end of the educational scale? How did our brightest young people do at college age after they'd been taught reading by look-and-say in first grade? For them, look-and-say worked like a time bomb. In 1963 the nationwide college entrance test (Scholastic Aptitude Test or SAT) scores began to drop. They've been dropping steeply ever since, with no end in sight. Verbal SAT averages, which stood at 478 in 1963, were down to 424 in 1980—a staggering drop of 9 percent of the whole 200-800-point range in seventeen years.

In 1977 a blue-ribbon twenty-one-member advisory panel, headed by former Secretary of Labor Willard Wirtz, issued a report on the decline in the SAT scores. "The panel members," it said, "share strongly the national concern about the increasing signs of functional illiteracy . . . [but they could find] no *one* cause of the SAT score decline."

However, in an appendix to the report, Professor Jeanne Chall of Harvard University offered a clue to that one basic cause. The students' low SAT scores, she wrote, had a "clearcut" statistical relationship to the reading instruction program used ten years earlier in first grade. The program had been based on a series of "look-and-say" readers.

There's little doubt that we'll soon have doctors who can't easily read medical journals, lawyers who have difficulty researching a case, scientists who stumble through their professional literature. In the 1990s we'll have to import top professionals from abroad. We'll join the ranks of such undereducated Third World countries as the Ivory Coast, Saudi Arabia, and Zambia. And there'll be few, if any, Nobel Prize winners who learned to read in an American school.

I've earned the right to say that these grim prospects are the direct results of look-and-say teaching in our schools. Twenty-five years ago I studied American methods of teaching reading and warned against educational catastrophe. Now it has happened.

Surely you don't want your Johnny or Mary to grow up as a functional illiterate or educational cripple. In this book I'll show you what you can do to help your child get a good education.

I'll start with the difference between phonics-first and look-and-say.

Learning to read is like learning to drive a car. You take lessons and learn the mechanics and the rules of the road. After a few weeks you've learned how to drive, how to stop, how to shift gears, how to park, and how to signal. You've also learned to stop at a red light and understand road signs. When you're ready, you take a road test, and if you pass, you can drive.

Phonics-first works the same way. The child learns the mechanics of reading, and when he's through, he can read.

Look-and-say works differently. The child is taught to read *before* he's learned the mechanics—the sounds of the letters. It's like learning to drive by starting your car and driving ahead. You'd learn to recognize and remember certain landmarks. First, on your street, you pass by the big yellow garage, the house with a plastic stork on the lawn, and the dentist's house. You turn right and pass the plumber, the florist, and the Italian restaurant. You turn again and drive by the stationery store, the carpenter, the podiatrist, the funeral home, and the bank. Then you come to the big intersection with the Exxon and the Texaco gas stations. You turn again and pass the diner, the gift shop, the drugstore, the optometrist, the little knit shop, and the pediatrician. One more turn and you're back home.

Continuing that "look-and-say" method of learning how to drive, you would repeat that lesson for three or four months until you'd be fully familiar with all the landmarks—the yellow garage, the plastic stork, the dentist, the plumber, the florist, the Italian restaurant, the stationery store, the carpenter, the podiatrist, the funeral home, the bank, the Exxon station, the Texaco station, the diner, the gift shop, the drugstore, the optometrist, the knit shop, and the pediatrician. You'd have learned to drive around the block.

Then you'd be allowed to go farther. Three months and you would have learned how to drive to the Catholic church and the supermarket. By the time you've fully learned those other landmarks, it would be the end of the school year and you would have a "landmark vocabulary" of 350 items. Next year you'd learn to drive to the railroad station and the Protestant church on the hill.

And the mechanics of driving? You'd pick those up as you go along. After three months you'd learn how to step on the brake, after another two months you'd learn how to signal. Next year you'd learn about traffic lights.

Now let's see how these two methods work with reading. With phonics-first the child is first taught the letters of the alphabet and what sounds they stand for. Since English has only twenty-six letters to express about forty-four sounds, this is done in a strict sequence so that the child sees only words whose letter sounds he has already learned. For instance, a sentence in the first Lippincott reader says, "Ann and Dan pin up the map." Before they get to that sentence, the children have learned the sounds of *n, d, p, m,* short *a,* short *i,* and short *u.* They've also learned the word *the,* one of a handful of special words taught out of sequence to make it possible to tell a story.

At the end of a semester or a year or two years, depending on which phonic system you use, children can read an estimated 24,000 words in their speaking or listening vocabulary. They can then go on to grammar, composition, literature, social studies, and science—in other words, they can start on their education.

And how does look-and-say work? It works on the principle that children learn to read by reading. It starts with little "stories" containing the most-often-used words in English and gradually builds up a "sight vocabulary." The children learn to read by seeing those words over and over again. By the end of first grade they can recognize 349 words, by the end of second grade 1,094, by the end of third grade 1,216, and by the end of fourth grade 1,554. (I got those numbers from the Scott, Foresman series, but all look-and-say series teach about the same number of words.)

The Scott, Foresman cumulative fourth-grade list contains the words *anteater, chariot, freckle, Hawaiian, laryngitis, peccary, Siberian, skunk,* and *toothpick.* But it does *not* contain the words *boil, cell, cheap, church, coal, cost, crime, due, fact, pain, pray, pride, puff, root, steam, stock, sum, tax, twelve,* and *vote.* These are words a look-and-say-trained child may *not* be able to read by the end of fourth grade. Of course, if he'd been taught phonics-first, he'd be able to read his full speaking or listening vocabulary, which has been estimated at 40,000 words.

Look-and-say readers still start the way they used to. I looked at a pre-primer of the 1979 Ginn 720 series and found myself right back in the early fifties. The same repetitive little "stories," the same children, the same dog. The dog's name is Lad, and the three white children, Bill, Jill, and Ben, have been joined by two black children, Ted and Nan, and by Rosa, who is Hispanic. But the stuff inside is much the same as it always was:

I am Rosa.
I am Lad.
Rosa runs.
Bill runs.
Lad and Rosa go.
Rosa and Jill go.
Go, Rosa, go.
Go, Bill, go.

There's one difference between the look-and-say readers of twenty-five years ago and those of today. Today they all offer some phonics. Not that they've gone over to the phonics-first camp, but since millions of parents now clamor for phonics, they give them a minimum of phonics—served up in a look-and-say sauce of "context clues" and guesswork.

Unfortunately, this bit of window dressing does the children no good at all. They still don't learn phonics *before* they learn the words spelled by the phonic rules. Instead, they get a little phonics that's too late, incomplete, thrown in more or less at random. Along with being taught to read those measly 1,500 words, they're taught some phonics as if it were a separate subject like math.

For instance, the first line in the 1978 Scott, Foresman look-and-say pre-primer says, "Look and Listen." When are the children taught the sound of double *o* as in *look? Two years later,* when they're in third grade. Lesson 10 in their third-grade reader starts, "When you see a word with the letters *oo . . .*"

And when do they learn about the silent *t* in listen? I plowed through the whole sixteen-volume Scott, Foresman series, but in vain. Silent *t* is never explained. Nor are *ph* and *qu*, even though the first-grade reader contains the words *elephant* and *queen*.

All look-and-say readers do the same thing. In the Ginn 720 series, page 36 of the first-grade reader is wholly devoted to teaching the word *this.* The phonic "explanation" of the word is given *one-and-a-half years later*, in second grade. How is it done? By asking the children to circle a word to complete the sentence "I like ^bath~this car best." (Phonics window dressing taught by a look-and-say "context clue.")

In another Ginn 720 first-grade book they teach the word *guess* by repeating it eight times in a 124-word story. And when does the Ginn series get around to teaching the sound of *gu* as in *guess, guest,* or *guide? Three years later*, in fourth grade.

Again, in a 1979 Houghton Mifflin first-grade reader, children learn the word *bus* early in the year. When are they taught the sound of short *u? One-and-a-half years later*, in second grade. Then the teacher is told to put the words *up, but, stuck,* and *lunch* on the blackboard and tell the children, "Listen for the vowel you hear in each word."

In the same second-grade reader, the children are taught to memorize the word *enough.* And when are they taught the *f* sound of *gh* in *enough, rough, tough,* and *laugh?* The answer is, Never. Houghton Mifflin simply doesn't bother with such trifles.

So, in spite of all the phonic window dressing, look-and-say still teaches reading by pictures, by telling what the word means, or simply by letting the children guess. Since all those methods have long been thoroughly discredited, they're disguised.

Instead of telling the children outright what a word means, teachers are told in a 1979 Harcourt Brace Jovanovich teacher's manual: "Write the word *buy* on the chalkboard. Point to the word and ask the children to pronounce it. If necessary, say '*Buy* begins like *boy* and rhymes with *why*.' "

Instead of referring the children to the picture of a king they have in front of them, teachers are told, in a Scott, Foresman manual: "Point to the word *king* and say, 'How do you know that this word is *king* and not *kitchen?*' " The children are supposed to answer "Because of the context," but of course they can tell by the picture.

A classic example of the look-and-say method is this instruction to teachers in a 1979 Houghton Mifflin third-grade manual:

> Print *disturb* on the board and say, "You can find out what this word is. I am going to say a sentence but leave out this word at the end. When I stop, use what you know about the sounds the letters stand for to help you think of a word that would make sense with the other words. Here's the sentence: When I went past my brother's bedroom, I noticed that his door was shut and there was a sign up saying, 'do not _____.' What is the word? . . . How do you know it isn't *disposal?* . . . ('*Disposal* doesn't make sense with what you said.') How do you know it isn't *interfere?* . . . ('*Interfere* doesn't begin with the sound that *d* stands for.')"

When I went to Teachers College, Columbia University, I was taught that the worst thing a teacher can do is suggest mistakes. But the look-and-say educators love this device. It's in all their teachers' manuals. For instance:

Print: *handkerchief*
Say: "He reached into his pocket and pulled out
           a _____."
Checking words: *handicap* (no sense)
                         wallet (wrong sounds)

Or this:

> Print: *salad*
> Say: "For lunch I ate a vegetable _____."
> Checking words: *salary* (no sense)
>   *casserole* (wrong sounds)

When I read this, my twenty-five-year-old anger came flooding back. Just think of it! At the end of *third grade* students are not expected to be able to read the word *salad. Salad!* A word that a phonics-first school teaches in the first weeks of first grade!

But the look-and-say educators don't care. They know full well that after three years their students are apt to read *salad* as *salary* or *casserole.* Why? Because they've kept it a closely guarded secret that the word *salad* can be read by sounding out the letters *s, a, l, a, d.*

Did I say three years? I'm sorry I misled you. Many look-and-say-taught children *never* catch on to the letter-sound relationships of the English language. I can prove this—right out of the horse's mouth.

The Houghton Mifflin series of readers runs from kindergarten through eighth grade. In 1978 the publishers realized that junior high school English teachers may not be aware of the abominable situation in the lower grades. They may naïvely assume that all their students can read.

To deal with this problem, Houghton Mifflin inserted a full-page, boldface statement opposite the title page in both their seventh- and eighth-grade teachers' manuals. The statement is called *An Important Statement Regarding the Decoding of Words Strange Only in Printed Form.* I quote:

> Some students have not yet learned how to decode easily and quickly the printed form of the language into the oral form with which they are thoroughly familiar. . . . They are probably not sufficiently aware that any specific reading passage consists of letter symbols in a sort of secret code. . . . They almost certainly lack mastery of a reliable strategy for decoding printed language. . . . For those students . . . provide the necessary instruction recommended on pages 455–458.

Translated into plain English, this means:

Perhaps, as a junior high school English teacher, you don't know that some students in your class have been taught by look-and-say and don't know how to read. Many of them have never caught on to the fact that letters stand for sounds. Please do the exercises in the back of this manual with them to help them learn to read.

Sure enough, in the back of the seventh- and eighth-grade manuals are some quite useless instructions on how to teach, *seven years too late,* such words as *demonstrated, rear, plumber, costume, gleam, stumbled, mending, pool,* and *brake.* The word *brake,* for instance, is to be taught this way:

Context: "The car began to roll down the hill. Think-
           ing quickly, Sally jumped into the car and
           put her foot on the *brake.*"
Questions: "How do you know the word is not *pedal?*"
           "How do you know the word is not *broom?*"

So now it's official. The leading look-and-say publisher has let the cat out of the bag. Millions of junior high school students, taught by look-and-say, can't distinguish the words *brake, pedal,* and *broom.*

The moral of all this is clear. Go to your child's school tomorrow morning and find out what system it uses to teach reading. Check the textbooks against these two lists:

THE PHONIC FIVE

1. Addison-Wesley Publishing Co., 2725 Sand Hill Road, Menlo Park, Calif. 94825
2. Distar, Science Research Associates, 259 East Erie Street, Chicago, Ill. 60611
3. Economy Company, 1901 North Walnut Street, Oklahoma City, Okla. 73125
4. J. B. Lippincott Company, East Washington Square, Philadelphia, Pa. 19105
5. Open Court Publishing Co., P.O. Box 599, La Salle, Ill. 61301

THE DISMAL DOZEN

1. Allyn & Bacon, Inc.
2. American Book Company
3. Ginn & Company
4. Harcourt Brace Jovanovich
5. Harper & Row
6. Holt, Rinehart & Winston
7. Houghton Mifflin Company
8. Laidlaw Brothers
9. Macmillan, Inc. (regular series)
10. Macmillan, Inc. (Bank Street Readers)
11. Riverside Publishing Co. (Rand McNally & Co.)
12. Scott, Foresman & Company

If the school uses one of the Phonic Five series, Johnny or Mary will be all right. They'll soon read better than most American children.

But if the school uses one of the Dismal Dozen, you have a problem. Johnny or Mary may never learn to read without fumbling and stumbling.

Here's what you can do about it.

To begin with, give Johnny first aid. Since he won't be taught phonics-first in school, teach him phonics at home.

Don't tell me you can't do it. It's only the look-and-say educators who have blown this thing out of all proportion and have made the teaching of reading seem like going to the moon. Actually, it's quite simple. All you need is a series of step-by-step exercises plus time and patience. Millions of nineteenth century Americans taught their children to read the same way with the aid of the famous little Webster's Blue-Backed Speller. Tens of thousands of mothers and fathers have done it successfully with the help of my book *Why Johnny Can't Read—And What You Can Do About It* (Harper & Row, 1955).

Of course you can do it. So can your parents, your older children, your twelve-year-old babysitter (if she's been taught phonics-first). I've taught each of my six children that way, each before he or she entered school, and those were among the happiest and most satisfying experiences of my life. It's an unforgettable moment when a child first discovers the key to the "secret code."

However, even if you teach your Johnny successfully at home, he'll still be exposed to the poor education he's getting at his look-and-say school. He'll go to school with lots of children who can't read. He'll learn from textbooks that were carefully "dumbed down" one, two, or more grades. He'll attend featherweight courses tailored to educational cripples. If possible, get him out of there and into a phonics-first school. Their number is growing, and if you're lucky, you'll find one not far from your home.

Don't think this suggestion is frivolous. I'm very serious about it. With our schools the way they are, this is possibly the most important thing you can do for your child's future career and happiness. If I had a child in a look-and-say school, I'd gladly have him bused thirty miles to be taught phonics-first.

But suppose you can't do that. What then? In that case I suggest you try to make your school switch from the Dismal Dozen to one of the Phonic Five.

You say you have never done such a thing? Well, there's always the first time to take a hand in community affairs. Become an active citizen. Go to the school board. Start hollering. Ring doorbells. Organize meetings. Where there's a will, there's a way. Thousands of parents throughout the nation have done it and so can you. Witness the famous case of the parents of Rochester, New York—black and white—who forced the city to adopt phonics-first readers. Dozens of other stories tell of parents who overcame a stubborn superintendent or won a majority on the school board—all to ensure that their children were taught phonics-first.

To give you an idea of what to expect if you succeed, I made arrangements to visit a phonics-first school. As soon as I contacted the five phonics publishers, I got lists of hundreds of schools that would be glad to have me visit their classrooms. (I wonder if any look-and-say schools proudly open their classrooms to observers of what's going on.)

To save time, I decided to visit a school nearby and picked at random a phonics-first school in New York City. Yes, I know what you're going to say. New York, as everyone knows, is an educational desert where reading test scores have been dropping year after year. But some ten years ago the city's school principals were at long last given a free hand and allowed to escape from the deadly grip of look-and-say. A few of them chose phonics-first and almost overnight made the desert bloom with educational "miracles."

One such school is P.S. 251, deep in the heart of Brooklyn. It serves the Paerdegat district, whose children are Irish, Italian, Jewish, black, Puerto Rican, Chinese, Korean, Haitian, Cuban—a great American ethnic mix.

I visited P.S. 251 in May 1979. The principal, Mrs. Cynthia Kamen, gave me a complete guided tour through a dozen or more classrooms. I saw a succession of "miracles"—only of course in a phonics-first school miracles happen every day. P.S. 251 uses the Open Court Publishing Company system and its pupils start to prepare for reading in kindergarten.

Each of the classrooms was filled with wide-awake, self-confident children. Each question produced a forest of eagerly raised hands.

I went into a kindergarten classroom. The children had learned the whole alphabet and treated me to rousing versions of the "H-song" and "W-song."

In first and second grade, the children proved to me that they could read anything. I had brought a list of six test words— *flamingo, curlicue, delicacy, inert, stoic,* and *squabble.* They read those words without trouble and pronounced them correctly.

Next I showed them a headline from that morning's *New York Times.* It said:

> *Senate Confirmation Role Sought*
> *On Posts of Brzezinski and Aide*

Out of five first- and second-graders I showed that headline to, four read and pronounced all the words correctly, including the name of President Carter's national security adviser. I remember particularly little Theresa in second grade, who rattled off the name as if it were her own.

My daughter Abby went with me on my trip to P.S. 251 and can testify under oath that these "miracles" actually happened.

Next, in a third-grade classroom, we listened to a bright boy named Steven reading aloud a story he'd written. Its first paragraph read:

> Gus is a flying hippo. He is big, fat, and klutzy. He is kelly green with lopsided spots. Just look for his crimson face peering at you. Last seen he was wearing a bright purple sweater. He talks like a hypochondriac.

Other third-graders read to us poems from the third-grade Open Court reader. They read "Daffodils" by William Wordsworth and "The Lost Shoe" by Walter de la Mare. They had no problems with Wordsworth's words *continuous, margin,* and *sprightly,* or with Walter de la Mare's references to Hindustan and Pernambuco.

The children in the fourth grade had read twenty books in the Random House Landmark series about historical figures and were eager to tell us about Benjamin Franklin and Clara Barton.

Then we looked in on a sixth grade, where the students were rehearsing a play. Among the books they'd read were plays by Thornton Wilder and William Saroyan, *Jane Eyre, Great Expectations,* and *The Diary of Anne Frank.*

We next went into a few classrooms where specially trained teachers tutored emotionally disturbed and learning-disabled children, transferred from other schools. They are taught with immense patience and loving attention to each child. Their progress is slow, but P.S. 251 simply doesn't tolerate nonreaders.

The school also has "magnet" classes for gifted children. We spent a happy quarter of an hour in a kindergarten filled with bright kids who read from a long list of outlandish words their teacher had taught them—words like *digressing, ecology, decorous,* and *dactylology.* I didn't know what that last word meant and the children explained to me that it meant hand-sign language. They also knew the definitions of all the other words. A *vow* meant "a promise," a *kleptomaniac* was "someone who steals and can't help it," a *phenomenon* was "like a miracle." When we came to the word *mandatory,* the teacher asked them whether kindergarten was mandatory. Happily they chorused, "No!!!"

It was 12:30 and we prepared to leave. But then Mrs. Kamen

casually mentioned a fourth-grade class whose teacher, Mrs. Mildred Cohen, taught a special unit about Greek mythology. *That* I had to see. So we went into the fourth-grade classroom. The children were asked to tell us the mythological stories they'd learned. Nine-year-old Mark told us with vim and vigor about Persephone, the daughter of Demeter, who went to Hades and brought back seven pomegranates. I interrupted Mark and asked him to spell *pomegranate*. He did so, hardly breaking his stride, and went on with his story. Next, charming little Shari told us about Prometheus stealing fire. She casually mentioned his obscure brother Epimetheus, pronouncing the name without the slightest hesitation.

Mrs. Cohen proudly gave us a collection of poems the children had written about the Greek gods. I particularly liked this one by nine-year-old Ruth:

> Nectar
> Zeus drinks nectar
> The Gods eat ambrosia
> The Gods live on Mount Olympus
> Way up

2

History of a Gimmick

When I wrote my book *Why Johnny Can't Read* twenty-five years ago, I wrote a chapter on the history of look-and-say, tracing it back to a primer called *The New Word Method,* published in 1846. I got that information from the book *American Reading Instruction* by Nila Banton Smith.

It turned out that Professor Smith and I were wrong. In 1966, eleven years after I wrote *Why Johnny Can't Read,* there appeared *Teaching to Read, Historically Considered* by Dr. Mitford M. Mathews, the famous linguist and editor of the monumental *Dictionary of Americanisms.* Dr. Mathews went into the matter with meticulous scholarship and settled it once and for all. The first look-and-say primer was written in 1791 by a German educator, Professor Friedrich Gedike, director of the Kölnische Gymnasium in Berlin.

Herr Professor Gedike was a fervent believer in the educational theories of Jean-Jacques Rousseau. He said teaching should follow nature. Nature presented Man with wholes—a flower, a tree, an animal, a mountain. To learn about those wholes, Man had to analyze what they were made of, going from the whole to its parts.

In an essay written in 1779 Gedike applied this idea to the teaching of reading. Reading instruction too, he wrote, should go from the whole—that is, the word—to its parts—the letters.

It took Gedike twelve years, till 1791, to translate this idea into a workable primer. It was called *Kinderbuch zur ersten Übung im Lesen ohne ABC und Buchstabieren,* which means "Children's Book for the First Practice in Reading without the ABC's and Spelling." He taught his five-year-old daughter with it and had her reading within two months.

Please note two things about this original look-and-say primer. First of all, it was aimed squarely at the market of affectionate middle-class parents. Ever since the invention of the alphabet 3,500 years ago, parents had been exasperated with the job of teaching their children to read. Small children simply hated to spend months on end in laboriously learning the ABC's, the standard first syllables *ba, be, bi, bo, bu,* and the seemingly endless drill they had to go through before they were allowed to read their first words. And yet this method had been in use for some 3,000 years simply because nobody had figured out any other way. So Gedike proudly called his primer a book "for the first practice in reading without the ABCs and spelling." Obviously he knew he was onto something.

How did he do it? He did it with a gimmick. Each page of his book had words containing one specific letter of the alphabet, say *m* or *f* or *b*. Each word was printed so that the letter to be learned stood out, printed in red, with the rest of the letters in black, or vice versa. When the child had learned the words on the page, presumably the featured letter had sunk in and would be remembered. By the end of the book the child had learned a long list of words and *incidentally* all the letters of the alphabet.

How would the child go on from there? How would he or she learn the rest of the tens of thousands of words in the German language? For this question Professor Gedike had an ingenious answer. "Don't think," he wrote in his preface, "that the child by this method knows only the words he has actually learned. . . . No! Through the mysterious sense of analogy he will increasingly find out words on his own or, if you will, *learn to guess.* At the same time, he will sense, even more mysteriously, why it must be this word and no other."

There you have it. In the world's first look-and-say book, the method is already exposed as a gimmick. No more torturous learning of the alphabet, no more boring syllable drills, simply teach the child a list of words and he'll "mysteriously" catch on to the sounds the letters stand for and learn to read on his own. Parents, save yourself and your child from unpleasantness and buy my book.

Only of course it turned out the gimmick didn't work. Little Gretchen Gedike (or whatever her name was) may have learned to read at her learned father's knee, but few other German children did so with his book. It went through three editions and then dropped from sight. Children in Germany and elsewhere kept on being drilled in the ABCs and *ba, be, bi, bo, bu.*

Some thirty years passed until the next look-and-say educator, Professor Jean Joseph Jacotot, arrived on the scene with *La Langue Maternelle* ("The Mother Tongue"). Monsieur Jacotot's method wasn't just a gimmick like Gedike's but a monstrosity.

Jacotot was a child prodigy. At nineteen he was appointed professor of Latin at the University of Dijon. He then studied law, practiced for a while, and also studied higher mathematics on the side. Then came the French Revolution. He joined the army, became an artillery captain and fought in the Belgian campaign. After the war he went back to Dijon and taught science, math, and Roman law. For a time he was a member of the French Parlement in Paris. After the Bourbons returned, he emigrated to Belgium and became Professor of French at the University of Louvain.

In 1823 he wrote the book *L'Enseignment universel* ("Universal Instruction"), which made him famous. One part of it dealt with the teaching of reading. There Jacotot went back to his experience in teaching Flemish-speaking university students how to speak and read French. He'd given them copies of the widely read French novel *Les Aventures de Télémaque* by Fénelon, in an edition printed in parallel columns, French on the left and Flemish on the right. Pretty soon Jacotot found that his students learned to read French by themselves.

Why not apply this principle to small children learning to read their native language? What Jacotot proposed, unbelievably, was this: Let the teacher read to the children the whole four-hundred-page novel *Télémaque*, several times if necessary. Then, when they have fully grasped the contents of the novel, start over again on page 1, read aloud the first sentence, and analyze it in detail, first the individual words and then each letter in each word. Once you have done this with every sentence in the book, the children know how to read. Incidentally, the first sentence of *Télémaque* was: "Calypso was unable to console herself for the departure of Ulysses."

German educators, always eager to apply new theories, tried the Jacotot method but found it a little cumbersome. Why not just use one sentence instead of a whole novel? they asked, with some justification. So, in 1830, there appeared the first German primer à la Jacotot by a German named Friedrich Weingart. Weingart's first sentence to be read and analyzed by the children was this:

> Socrates, the wise son of Sophroniscus, spoke one day in the circle of his students of the all-powerful foresight of divine providence—how it sees everything and hears everything and is present everywhere and takes care of everything, and how a man the more he feels and recognizes it the more he honors it.

Other German educators felt that Weingart's opening sentence was a trifle long, so they came out with primers starting with shorter sentences and finally with primers starting with single words. The children were taught those words *and what each letter in each word stood for.* This was the beginning of the German "Normal Word method," which soon conquered Germany and all of Europe. In essence, it's what we today call phonics.

Around the time Jacotot made his big splash in Europe, an American, Thomas H. Gallaudet, reinvented the look-and-say method in the United States.

Gallaudet had for many years been working with deaf mutes. He had developed a purely visual method of teaching them to read and felt it could and should also be used in teaching normal children. What he had done was this: he'd put fifty words like *horse, dog, cat* on little cards, let the children memorize them by sight, and then taught them the letters by analyzing the words. In 1836 he published his invention under the title *A Mother's Primer.*

Other authors—Josiah Bumstead, John Russell Webb, and Samuel Worcester—also came out with look-and-say primers around the same time. They didn't have such an unusual background but the principle was the same. Each of those primers started with a lengthy list of words to be learned during the first weeks of school before the children were set to work on letters and the alphabet.

Another author of a new look-and-say primer was Mrs. Mary Peabody Mann, the second wife of the famous educator Horace Mann. Her book didn't mention the alphabet or letters at all, but that didn't stop her husband from giving it a friendly review. "It is a beautiful book," he wrote. "It is prepared on the same general principles with those of Worcester, Gallaudet, and Bumstead; and it contains two or three reading lessons and a few cuts for drawing, in addition to a most attractive selection of words."

In 1843 Mann went with his wife to Europe and spent an hour in a Prussian classroom during a reading lesson. Although he didn't know a word of German, his wife interpreted for him what was happening. Nevertheless, he misunderstood completely what the teacher was doing—he was using the by then standard "normal word method"—and thought this was a demonstration of look-and-say.

When he came back to the United States, Mann wrote his famous Seventh Annual Report to the Massachusetts Board of Education and recommended passionately the use of look-and-say. He wrote about the methods used by Gallaudet, Bumstead, Worcester, his wife, and the Prussian schoolteacher, mixing it all together in a frontal attack on the prevailing method of teaching children with the alphabet and *ba, be, bi, bo, bu.*

A committee of thirty-one Boston grammar school masters came up with a lengthy answer, insisting that look-and-say produced very poor spellers and anyway didn't work when it came to reading unfamiliar words.

Within a few years after that "great debate" in Massachusetts, the various look-and-say primers went out of fashion and the alphabetic or phonic methods kept on being used in the nation's classrooms.

A quarter century passed. Then, almost unnoticed, look-and-say made a reappearance. In 1881, Mr. George L. Farnham, principal of the State Normal School in Peru, Nebraska, wrote a small book, *The Sentence Method of Teaching Reading, Writing, and Spelling.* It achieved a certain underground fame and went into three editions.

Farnham went beyond the earlier look-and-say proponents and suggested that children should start their reading and writing lessons with whole sentences. "The teacher goes to the board," he wrote, "and in a clear bold hand writes a sentence, as: 'I have a knife.' The pupils see the writing, but of course do not know what it means. The teacher will call a pupil and put a knife into his hands, and the pupil in response to the impulse which is the result of previous training will instantly hold up the knife and say 'I have a knife.' "

And so on, until the children "attain great excellence in writing and reading at an early period."

As to the letters, "the teacher will speak of the letters as though they were known to the pupils, showing the size of the *m*'s, *t*'s, *l*'s etc., and it will soon be discovered that the pupils can distinguish the letters and name them." So much for that.

Far from being ridiculed, Farnham's method was soon widely imitated, and many publishers put out sentence- or story-method primers. One of them was the Elson Readers of the Scott, Foresman Company in Chicago, to which I'll return a little later.

And now the curtain goes up for the entrance of the great national leader of look-and-say, Colonel Francis Wayland Parker.

Parker was a great big bear of a man with a booming voice, a hearty laugh, and an abiding love for little children. He started as superintendent of public schools in Quincy, Massachusetts, and soon became nationally famous. In 1883 the city of Chicago called him in as principal of the Cook County Normal School.

Parker's ideas on educational reform are explained in his book *Talks on Pedagogics*. On the subject of reading he said:

From the time the child first enters school, the purpose of the teacher should be to continue in the best possible way the spontaneous activities of the child in the directions which nature has so effectively begun. We will suppose, then, that he has lessons, experiments, observations, and investigations in all the central subjects; that they form the core of the work done by the teacher; that the child's mind, his whole being, is brought face to face with the truth,—the intrinsic knowledge,—and consequently with intrinsic thought; and that at the moment when the word is required, it is given orally, and at once written rapidly, in a plain, beautiful hand upon the blackboard. . . .

It is easy for a skillful teacher to arouse an intense interest in an educative subject. Just at the moment when the interest is at its height, she introduces a word orally, immediately writes it upon the blackboard, erases it, after one glance by her pupils, and says, "Say that with the chalk!" The little ones rush to the board, under a strong desire to express the thought, and quickly reproduce the word.

After some sixteen years of this kind of teaching the Cook County Board of Education had had enough and Parker had to resign his post. But at that critical moment the look-and-say movement was rescued by Mrs. Anita McCormick Blaine.

Mrs. Blaine was the daughter of Cyrus McCormick, inventor of the harvesting machine, and an heiress to the McCormick fortune. She was deeply interested in educational reforms. When her son, Emmons junior, reached the age of six and had to start on his education, she looked carefully for the proper kind of school to send him to. When she heard of Colonel Parker, she visited his school and asked to see one of the reading classes. Parker proudly answered, "We haven't any," and Mrs. Blaine was instantly overwhelmed. When he lost his job a few years later, she contributed a million dollars to set up a new school for him under the wing of the University of Chicago. It became world-famous and attracted pilgrimages from progressive educators everywhere.

But let's go on. The next hero of the look-and-say movement is Edmund Burke Huey, author of *The Psychology and Pedagogy of Reading,* which appeared in 1908. It instantly became the bible of the movement.

Huey went over the whole history of the alphabet, writing, and reading, and included a complete survey of how reading was taught in America at that time. On the basis of his psychological theory, he came out squarely for look-and-say teaching à la Parker, only if possible more so. At the end of his book he summed it all up in thirteen "practical pedagogical conclusions." The first four were:

1. The home is the natural place for learning to read, in connection with the child's introduction to literature through story-telling, picture-reading, etc. . . .
2. The school should cease to make primary reading the fetish that it long has been, and should construct a primary course in which reading and writing will be learned secondarily, and only as they serve a purpose felt as such by the pupil, the reading being always for meaning.
3. The technique of reading should not appear in the early years, and the very little early work that should be tolerated in phonics should be entirely distinct from reading.
4. The child should never be permitted to read for the sake of reading, as a formal process or end in itself. The reading should always be for the intrinsic interest or value of what is read, reading never being done or thought of as "an exercise." Word-pronouncing will therefore always be secondary to getting whole sentence-meanings, and this from the very first.

On the question of what the children are supposed to read, point 13 contained an illuminating sentence:

The literature of Teutonic feudalism and chivalry and of medieval romanticism seems especially suited to the nature and interests of adolescents.

Having unburdened himself of this strange new gospel on how to teach reading, Huey turned away from the field and went back to his first love, work with the mentally deficient. He spent the next five years preparing a book on that subject, but the manuscript was completely destroyed by fire. He died at the age of forty-three in 1913.

What with the fame of the Parker school and the wide influence of Huey's book, look-and-say now began to come into its own. More and more private schools adopted the system, and an ever-increasing number of publishers brought out texts to serve the movement. In New York City, Columbia University

Teachers College embraced look-and-say together with progressive education, and the University of Chicago and other institutions followed suit.

The two foremost leaders were Professor Arthur I. Gates of Columbia and Professor William S. Gray at Chicago. In 1929 the Scott, Foresman Company invited Professor Gray to revamp their Elson Readers, and this marked the birth of Dick and Jane. A year later, Professor Gates joined up with Macmillan and produced a look-and-say series for them. Gradually most major textbook houses fell in line and the "Dismal Dozen" of basal readers came into being.

By the middle thirties look-and-say had completely swept the field. Virtually all leading academics in the primary reading field were now authors of basal reader series and collected fat royalties. They had inherited the kingdom of American education.

Inevitably that huge bonanza created problems. Look-and-say, after all, was still essentially a gimmick with no scientific foundations whatever. As it had for 150 years, it produced children who couldn't accurately read unfamiliar words. From the fourth grade up, textbooks in all subjects had to be "dumbed down" to accommodate them. Grade promotions had to be based on age rather than achievement. High school diplomas were given to functional illiterates. Colleges had to adjust to an influx of students who couldn't read. The national illiteracy rate climbed year after year after year.

The educational Establishment, with primary reading at its core, became a beleaguered fortress. In 1956 the International Reading Association was founded, and began to function as a look-and-say defense league. It now has over 65,000 members and publishes *three* journals, *The Reading Teacher, The Journal of Reading* and *The Reading Research Quarterly*. They're filled with articles defending the indefensible system of teaching reading.

This national tragedy was followed by high comedy. In the early sixties, after the original standard-bearers of look-and-say had died or retired, a new generation of academics took over. Look-and-say became "psycholinguistics" and reading mistakes became "miscues." Professor Frank Smith and Professors Kenneth and Yetta Goodman invented a new science to clothe shabby old look-and-say in shiny new garments.

Let's first have a look at Professors Kenneth and Yetta Goodman. They are husband and wife; he's now senior author of the Scott, Foresman series, having inherited the mantle of William S. Gray.

Professor Kenneth Goodman defines reading as "a psycholinguistic process by which the reader reconstructs, as best he can, a message which has been encoded by a writer as a graphic display."

Note the words "as best he can." Goodman, surrounded by two generations of look-and-say-trained Americans, assumes as a matter of course that everybody makes mistakes all the time. These mistakes he calls miscues—"in order to avoid value implications," as he puts it.

You'd think the fact that most Americans no longer can read accurately is deplorable. But the Goodmans don't feel that way. They first started a Reading Miscue Center at Wayne State University in Detroit, and then produced a brand-new, highly expensive, diagnostic reading test, The Miscue Reading Inventory—to be given to individual children orally. Naturally, this takes vastly more time and money than conventional written tests given to groups, but this is considered unimportant.

Educational journals are full of studies of how to apply the Miscue Reading Inventory. For instance, in the April 1978 issue of *Reading Teacher,* Professor Dixie Lee Spiegel writes:

> The development of confidence and risk-taking strategies within children can only evolve in a climate of acceptance and encouragement in which the students are rewarded for a good try. Children should be encouraged to take a risk and to make a good guess, using all the data that are available and that they know how to use. They should receive praise for a good guess even though it is not completely accurate. For example, if a child reads "I like to eat carrots" as "I like to eat cake," praise should be given for supplying a word that makes sense and follows at least some of the phonic cues. The teacher may also choose to supply the correct response in an offhand and uncritical manner. If the child read the sentence as

"I like to eat cars," the teacher should remind the reader that that does not make sense.

I could easily fill this book with similar examples of current scholarship in the field of reading instruction, but this will give you a good idea of what's going on. For the look-and-say educators reading is now a matter of "guessing," "cues," "strategies"—never of simply looking at what's on the page and, if necessary, sounding out the words. Professor Kenneth Goodman even wrote a paper called "Reading: A Psycholinguistic Guessing Game," which was reprinted several times in college anthologies.

Not long ago, in the November 1979 issue of the magazine *Learning*, a Goodman disciple summed it all up. Mr. Barry Sherman, a reading consultant in private practice, offered the following advice to students:

> Always try to make sense of everything you read.
> When you come to a word or phrase you don't know, guess that it is a word or phrase that looks like the one in the text and that has the meaning called for in the sentence.
> If you can't think of a word or phrase that looks like the one in the text, choose something that has the meaning you seem to need and read on.
> If you must skip a word, say "blank" and go on reading.
> When you come to an unfamiliar name of a person, recognize what kind of word it is, then choose a substitute name for the character and stick to it.
> When you come to phrases that tell who is talking, such as "she whispered," "he exclaimed" and "they replied," you can always use the word *said* in place of *whispered, exclaimed* and *replied*. The important thing is to keep reading.
> If you cannot figure out the meaning of a word, try to decide if it is a name of something or if it tells what something is, has or does; then keep reading.

On July 9, 1973, Professor Kenneth Goodman made his miscue theory nationally famous by giving an interview to the

New York Times. The interviewer asked him: "A student learning to read comes upon the sentence 'The boy jumped on the horse and rode off.' But instead of saying 'horse,' the student substitutes 'pony.' Should the teacher correct him?

Professor Goodman's answer was a firm no.

"The child clearly understands the meaning," he said. "This is what reading is all about."

What Professor Goodman apparently didn't know is that the *Merck Manual,* the standard reference source for doctors, lists as one of the symptoms of dyslexia—also called "congenital word blindness" or "primary reading disability"— the "tendency to substitute words for those he cannot read."

And now, to finish this chapter, let me introduce you to the apostle of psycholinguistics, Professor Frank Smith. Smith is a charismatic leader in the direct line of Parker and Huey. He has written three books, *Understanding Reading* (1971), *Psycholinguistics and Reading* (1973), and *Reading Without Nonsense* (1979). They all preach the same gospel, but as the years went by and Smith acquired a fanatic following, his books became less textbooky and more inspirational. *Reading Without Nonsense* no longer has any footnotes, bibliography, or other customary scholarly apparatus. It's pure Smith, one glittering paradox after another. Listen:

> Skill in reading depends on using the eyes as little as possible. (page 9)
>
> Meaning is not something that a reader or listener *gets from* language, but something that is *brought to* language. (page 9)
>
> If you are not making errors when you read, you are probably not reading efficiently. (page 33)
>
> When we identify meaning in text, it is not necessary to identify individual words. (page 117)

However, the most amusing passage in Smith's book is not one of those paradoxes, but the following (from pages 51–52):

> *The Fallacy of Phonics:* The issue concerns the number and nature of the correspondence between the letters of the written language and the sounds of speech. There would be a perfect "one-to-one correspondence" between

the two aspects of language if every letter stood for just one sound and every sound was represented by just one letter. Then indeed we might help children to read by getting them to learn the rules of spelling-to-sound correspondence. In the same mechanical way we could also employ computers to convert written language into speech to the great advantage of the blind. . . . The reason phonics does not work for children or for computers is that the links between the letters and sounds cannot be specified. . . . They are too complex."

This would be a splendid argument against phonics except for the awkward fact that the first Kurzweil Reading Machine was publicly demonstrated on January 13, 1976. It used a phonics-based program fed into a computer. There are now two hundred such machines in use in forty-eight states, England, Australia, and Canada.

The other day I listened to a Kurzweil machine in New York City read a page or two from a book on American history. It has an indefinable, vaguely foreign-sounding accent, but that only adds to the sheer awe-inspiring magic of its performance.

3

Look-and-Say Exposed

Mitford Mathews, the wise old author of *Teaching to Read, Historically Considered,* wrote:

> Those who have maintained the superiority of the word method as a way of teaching a child quickly have often succeeded in promoting themselves professionally, but they have not always enhanced their reputations as scholarly persons in the estimation of scholars in other disciplines. The fact is that the method, prior to its adoption, had never been scientifically tested in competition with any other. This assertion will be challenged by many devoted practitioners. All anyone has to do to refute it, however, is to give the details of the experiment: who conducted it, for how long, involving how many children, how many teachers, and so forth.

Mathews didn't mean, of course, that no such studies have been made. On the contrary, since the first was done in 1911 there have been *124* such studies, carefully comparing the results of phonics-first and look-and-say. How many of them proved the superiority of look-and-say? Not one—not a single, blessed one.

This sounds unbelievable, I know. In fact, it *is* unbelievable, considering the near-monopolistic rule of look-and-say for the past fifty or sixty years of American education. Nevertheless it's true. I can prove it by citing chapter and verse. If any educator wants to cite a single contrary research finding, he or she is welcome to do so.

Here are the facts:

When I wrote my book *Why Johnny Can't Read* in 1955, I

listed eleven studies that had been done up to that time. All of them gave results in favor of phonics-first; not a single one favored look-and-say. The scientific proof was complete and overwhelming.

Ten years later, in April 1965, Dr. Louise Gurren of New York University and Mrs. Ann Hughes, research director of the Reading Reform Foundation, published an article in the *Journal of Educational Research* called "Intensive Phonics vs. Gradual Phonics in Beginning Reading: A Review." It listed thirty-six studies, including most of those I had listed ten years before. Gurren and Hughes concluded:

1. Rigorous controlled research clearly favors teaching of all the main sound-symbol relationships, both vowel and consonant, from the start of formal reading instruction.
2. Such teaching benefits comprehension as well as vocabulary and spelling.
3. Phonetic groups are usually superior in grades 3 and above.

Two years later, in 1967, Professor Jeanne Chall of the Harvard University Graduate School of Education published her book *Learning to Read: The Great Debate*. It was based on five years of research, funded by a large Carnegie Foundation grant.

Professor Chall reviewed eighty-five studies, including most of those surveyed earlier by Gurren and Hughes and me. She not only surveyed classroom studies, but also laboratory and clinical studies of all kinds—anything that compared phonics-first (or "systematic phonics," "intensive phonics" or, in her terms, "code emphasis") with look-and-say (or "incidental phonics," "gradual phonics," "delayed phonics," or, in her term, "meaning emphasis"). Her conclusions are stated on page 307:

> My review of the research from the laboratory, the classroom and the clinic points to the need for a correction in beginning reading instructional methods. Most school children in the United States are taught to read by what I have termed a meaning-emphasis method. Yet, the research from 1912 to 1965 indicates that a code-emphasis

method—i.e. one that views beginning reading as essentially different from mature reading and emphasizes learning of the printed code for the spoken language—produces better results, at least up to the point where sufficient evidence seems to be available, the end of third grade.

The results are better, not only in terms of the mechanical aspects of literacy alone, as was once supposed, but also in terms of the ultimate goal of reading instruction—comprehension and possibly even speed of reading. The long-existing fear that an initial code-emphasis produces readers who do not read for meaning or with enjoyment is unfounded. On the contrary, the evidence indicates that better results in terms of reading for meaning are achieved with the programs that emphasize code at the start than with the programs that stress meaning at the beginning.

The fourth review of the evidence was done in 1973 by Dr. Robert Dykstra, professor of education at the University of Minnesota. It appeared as a fifty-page special section in the book *Teaching Reading* by Walcutt, Lamport, and McCracken. Dr. Dykstra reviewed fifty-nine studies, again partly overlapping the reviews by me, Gurren and Hughes, and Chall. He summarized the evidence on page 397:

Reviewing the research comparing (1) phonic and look-say instruction programs, (2) intrinsic and systematic approaches to helping children learn the code, and (3) code-emphasis and meaning-emphasis basal programs leads to the conclusion that children get off to a faster start in reading if they are given early direct systematic instruction in the alphabetic code. The evidence clearly demonstrates that children who receive early intensive instruction in phonics develop superior word recognition skills in the early stages of reading and tend to maintain their superiority at least through the third grade. . . .

We can summarize the results of 60 years of research dealing with beginning reading instruction by stating that early systematic instruction in phonics provides the child with the skills necessary to become an independent reader at an earlier age than is likely if phonics instruction is delayed and less systematic. As a consequence of his early success in "learning to read" the child can more quickly go about the job of "reading to learn."

The total count of the studies surveyed in the four overlapping research reviews is 116. There were 7 later studies that showed the superiority of the Distar phonic system over others in the federally funded Follow Through project, plus one important phonics-vs.-look-and-say study by Dr. Douglas Carnine, published in 1977, to which I'll return. This brings the total count to 124. As I said, *not one* of those 124 studies showed results favoring look-and-say.

Most of the 124 studies followed a simple pattern. The researcher compared two groups of children. One was trained by look-and-say, the other by phonics-first. At the end of the year, both groups were tested to find out which had progressed further in word recognition and comprehension.

To take just one example, in February 1958 the *Journal of Educational Research* published a study by Barbara C. Kelly, entitled "The Economy Method Versus the Scott, Foresman Method in Teaching Second-Grade Reading in the Murphysboro Public Schools." Miss Kelly had studied the reading achievement of 100 second graders in Murphysboro, Illinois, who'd been trained by the Economy Readers (one of my "Phonic Five" listed on page 9) and another group of 100 second graders trained by Scott, Foresman (one of the "Dismal Dozen"). She found a significant difference in favor of the phonics-trained children.

In this way, the 124 studies compared most of the available phonics-first materials with virtually all the Dismal Dozen look-and-say methods. The results invariably favored phonics.

In the early years, many of the experiments were done with the phonics readers put out by the Economy Company. After 1963, when the Lippincott Readers were first published, much experimentation was done with Lippincott material. For instance, there were a number of studies within the framework of 27 cooperative studies sponsored by the U.S. Office of Education in the mid-sixties. Lippincott won all the "races" in which it was entered.

The next major group of competitive studies was the massive Follow Through project, again sponsored by the federal government. It was designed to compare the results of various educational methods with disadvantaged children who had gone through preschool preparation with Head Start. The only phonics-first program entered in that "race" was Distar (also listed among my "Phonic Five" on page 9). Distar came out ahead in all the "races" it was entered in.

At the end of third grade *all children made gains in IQ from 6 to 8 points, and low-IQ children, with an average IQ of 73, gained between 8 and 14 points.* The participating schools were in Uvalde, Texas (90 percent Chicano); Tupelo, Mississippi; Flint, Michigan; Dayton, Ohio; and East St. Louis, Illinois (all four mostly black); and Flippin, Arkansas, and Smithville, Tennessee (both mostly white). All children in the program came from low-income families.

Beginning in the sixties, educational researchers also did a series of laboratory experiments to test the effectiveness of look-and-say. Their first order of business was the refutation of the famous Cattell study of 1885.

Cattell's study had been used over and over again by look-and-say educators to lend their gimmick some shred of respectability. Cattell had proved, they said, that we read whole words rather than letters and that therefore look-and-say is better than phonics.

Let's go back for a moment and see exactly what Dr. James McKeen Cattell did in 1885. He worked in a laboratory in Leipzig (most psychological laboratory work in those days was done in Germany), and tested readers with a tachistoscope, an instrument that exposes reading matter for a split second.

He found, to his surprise, that readers could read whole words in less time than it took them to read single letters. "These results are important enough," he wrote, "to prove those to be wrong who with Kant hold that psychology can never become an exact science."

Important, but wrong. The obvious flaw in the experiment was that Cattell tested only adults. (The group he used included one nine-year-old boy, but he "was superior in reading ability to some of the adults.")

Until 1965 nobody bothered to check his assumption that

beginning readers read the way fluent adult readers do. Then Drs. Gabrielle Marchbanks and Harry Levin of Cornell University decided to look into the matter. They took 50 kindergartners and 50 first graders and asked them to pick from a group of nonsense words the one most like another nonsense word they'd been shown. For instance, they were shown first the nonsense word *cug*, and then the four nonsense words *arp* (same shape), *che* (same first letter), *tuk* (same second letter), and *ilg* (same third letter.)

The results were clear. Most of the children went by the first letter, a smaller number by the last letter, and only a few by the general shape of the whole word.

Five years later, in 1970, Dr. Henry G. Timko repeated the Marchbanks-Levin experiment and came to the same conclusion—first graders recognize words by the first letter and *not* by the shape of the whole word.

In the same year, 1970, Drs. Joanna P. Williams, Ellen L. Blumberg, and David V. Williams repeated the experiment once more. They tested kindergartners, first-graders and adults. Their kindergartners used whole-word shape not at all, the first graders did it very rarely, and the adults only sometimes. After eighty-five years, the ghost of James Cattell had at long last been laid to rest.

"In view of these and other findings," Dr. Williams wrote, "there seems to be no justification for developing instructional methods or materials based on the use of configuration as the primary cue. . . . It is worth noting that the most widely used reading method over the past 30 years (the 'look-say' or 'whole word' method) has stressed identification of words on the basis of configuration."

At the same time that they disposed of Cattell's century-old error, researchers also established *why* phonics-first worked and look-and-say did not. What it all boils down to, they said, is the problem of "transfer of training." Which was more effective in learning to read unfamiliar printed words—memorizing whole words or learning letters and sounds?

The first experiment to solve this problem was done in 1964 by Miss Carol H. Bishop, then a graduate student at Cornell University working under Dr. Eleanor Gibson. Miss Bishop picked 60 college freshman and sophomores and taught 20 of them the sounds of twelve Arabic letters and another 20 the sounds of eight words composed of those letters. All students were then asked to try to read eight different Arabic words, containing the same eight letters.

Miss Bishop's results showed clearly that letter training was better than word training. What's more, when Miss Bishop analyzed her findings, she found that only those word-trained students who had figured out the sound values of the letters were able to learn the unfamiliar words. Which means that they knew about the alphabetic code in English and applied that knowledge to the job of learning Arabic words.

After three years, in 1967, a similar experiment was conducted by Drs. W. E. Jeffrey and S. Jay Samuels, then at the University of California in Los Angeles. Instead of adults, Jeffrey and Samuels took 60 kindergartners from a public school, and instead of Arabic characters they used arbitrary, odd-shaped symbols. The children in the word group were taught four nonsense words—*mo, so, ba, be,* and those in the letter group were taught the sounds of *s, m, a,* and *e.* The words to be learned were *se, sa, me* and *ma.*

Jeffrey and Samuels's results were the same as Miss Bishop's. The letter-trained group was clearly superior to the word-trained group.

Ten years later, in 1977, Dr. Douglas W. Carnine of the University of Oregon conducted another similar experiment. He tried to make the situation as much as possible like a classroom situation. So he used regular English letters, gave the children more words and letters to learn, and added some irregular words to those to be learned. Carnine's results confirmed those of Bishop and Jeffrey and Samuels. Phonics-first won hands-down over look-and-say.

Both the Jeffrey and Samuels experiment and Carnine's recapitulation had an important added feature—the letter-trained children were taught not only what sounds the letters stood for but also how to "blend" those sounds—saying *mmm* and *ee* and then blending them together to say *me.*

This special training in blending was based on the idea that learning tasks must be analyzed to find their component subskills. Then these subskills must be taught in a strict sequence— a hierarchy. A higher subskill in such a sequence is taught only when the lower subskill has been fully mastered. Only this way can a complex skill be taught so that it can be performed without mistakes.

The first psychologist to write about "task analysis," "subskills," and "learning hierarchies" was Dr. Robert M. Gagné. Dr. Gagné is not a reading expert but a psychologist specializing in the techniques of teaching and learning.

I wrote to Dr. Gagné and asked him how he first developed his idea. He answered:

> My ideas about task analysis, learning hierarchies and subordinate skills came originally from a study I did on the learning of ninth graders in a mathematics problem (inferring and stating a general formula for the sum of terms in a number series). When I ran across some students who seemed to be having particular difficulty learning to perform this task, it seemed to me they were missing some "subordinate skills," in some cases rather simple arithmetic skills. Accordingly, I did a study in which I first analyzed the subordinate skills of the number-series task, then tested students on them, and taught them the subordinate skills they didn't know. As a research psychologist used to the notion that learning is a gradual process, I was surprised by the results. Once subordinate skills were mastered, the new learning was very rapid, and "sudden."

In 1965 Dr. Gagné developed the first subskills hierarchy for the teaching of reading. It appears in the first edition of his widely used textbook *The Conditions of Learning.* Pointedly ignoring the commonly used look-and-say method, Dr. Gagné proposed a phonics-first method. Children were to be taught first the language sounds, then "recognition of printed letters by sound," then "recognition of printed words," then the "distinguishing of similar words," and so on.

> The objective at this stage of learning [Gagné wrote] is to enable the child to say orally such a word as *concatenation,* which he has never seen or heard before. Whether he knows the meaning of the word is quite irrelevant. The all-important capability he is acquiring at this stage

is the ability to say, when he sees it in print, the word *concatenation* in a way that is discriminably different *to him* from the printed word *concentration.* . . .

In an adult, the difficulties experienced with a novel word provide a fairly sure clue to the existence of a gap in his early instruction. . . . On the first encounter, he may be unable to read a word like *obsequiousness,* which, to an individual who has learned to identify sounds, is ridiculously simple.

The difference between phonics-first and look-and-say has hardly ever been stated more clearly. Look-and-say-trained children can't read because a vital step in their instruction—distinguishing between different spelling patterns—has been left out. Dr. Gagné, with his background in math and science, looked at the situation with unconfused eyes and pointed straight at the source of the trouble.

Gagné's subskill approach soon swept the field of reading research. It became the accepted doctrine among almost all reading researchers that decoding—that is, phonics-first—must be taught by a carefully worked-out sequence of subskills.

In a fascinating paper published in 1976, Dr. S. Jay Samuels, now at the University of Minnesota, compared the method with the teaching of a number of other complex skills.

Replying to Professor Frank Smith, who had written that one learns to read by reading just as one learns to ride a bicycle by riding a bicycle, Dr. Samuels said this isn't necessarily the way one learns to ride a bicycle either. "Children often go through a graded series of experiences of increasing difficulty before they learn to ride a large-frame, two-wheel bike. They frequently practice first on a tricycle, then graduate to a two-wheeler with a small frame, and practice getting their balance on the small frame bike before they use the pedals on their two-wheeler."

Or, Samuels continued, take the current method of teaching downhill skiing. "Perhaps the most significant recent advance has been with the GLM, graduated length method. The beginning skier uses short skis to practice his basic moves and then advances to longer skis as skill develops."

Or take training in wrestling. "Every move in wrestling is

broken down into its parts and the athlete practices these parts prior to putting them together to form a move that has fluid motion. When a move is finally mastered, combinations of moves are worked together to form larger units or patterns of moves."

Finally, Samuels mentioned the learning of dance steps.

> The trick in learning a new dance step without the aid of a teacher is to try to identify the basic move from which the variations originate. What the teacher does to simplify learning a dance is to select the basic step and to teach the subskills that comprise the basic step. Years ago the Arthur Murray system used this procedure to introduce people to social dancing. Their basic step was called the box step and was used to introduce a number of dances as well as their variations.

This is the system that Samuels and most other reading researchers now apply to the teaching of beginning reading. Samuels proposed a sequence of subskills going from learning distinctive letter features—like the differences between *b* and *d* or *p* and *q*—to letters, to letter clusters and on to words. Dr. Joanna Williams of Teachers College, Columbia University, and Drs. Michael and Lise Wallach of Duke University have added two steps *before* learning letter shapes, namely, learning to analyze in general, and learning to analyze spoken words into their component sounds. Higher up in the scale, children are taught to blend letters and sounds and to "chunk" such units as *str* or *ight*. Many scholars are now interested in carrying this approach higher and higher into more complex reading skills, such as comprehension and inference.

As you see, phonics-first, or decoding, is now the center of attention and the area that is of foremost interest to scholars. The Goodman and Smith type of guessing game is taking a backseat.

In the fall of 1979 there appeared a three-volume set of books called *Theory and Practice of Early Reading*. It contained scholarly papers by fifty-nine contributors, assembled and edited by Dr. Lauren Resnick of the University of Pittsburgh and Dr. Phyllis Weaver of Harvard University. There *are* papers by Drs. Kenneth and Yetta Goodman and Dr. Frank Smith and three of their followers. The fifty-three other contributors—about 90 percent—write mainly about decoding, or phonics-first.

Theory and Practice of Early Reading is a galaxy of today's academic stars in the field of reading research. It shows vividly where we are now. "In a sense," writes Dr. Resnick in her introduction, "these volumes are a reexamination of issues considered by Chall a decade ago" (that is, the "great debate" between phonics-first and look-and-say). "Somewhat modified basal reading approaches are still dominant in today's instructional practice, and they are even less favorably viewed by our contributors than they were by Chall."

"As a matter of routine practice," Dr. Resnick writes later in a summary article, "we need to include systematic, code-oriented instruction in the primary grades, no matter what else is also done."

Two outspoken contributors, Drs. Isabelle Y. Liberman and Donald Shankweiler of the University of Connecticut, write:

> Instructional procedures should inform children early on that the printed word is a model of the component phonemes [sounds] and their particular succession in the spoken word. . . . The instruction should not, as it often does, mislead children into assuming that the printed word is an ideographic symbol, a notion that will have to be corrected later and, apparently for some children, with great difficulty. Procedures that initiate children into the mystique of reading by drawing their attention to the visual configuration ("remember this shape; it has a 'tail' ") and its associated meaning ("the one with the tail means monkey") without alerting them to the relevance of the sound structure of the word may lead them into a blind alley. Their ability to memorize the shapes and associated meanings of a handful of words may lull them and their parents into the comfortable belief that they can read, but it may leave them stranded at that stage, functional illiterates with no keys to unlock new words.

Dr. S. Jay Samuels of the University of Minnesota writes:

> I had an opportunity to discuss what was needed to improve the teaching of reading with Tom Sticht, John

Guthrie, Harry Singer and Dennis Fisher. There was con-
sensus that at the present time a sufficient amount is
known about practical aspects of reading so that all children, even those at risk [the lowest 15 percent on the
IQ scale] can be taught to read. The problem, then, is
not a lack of knowledge about how to teach reading. The
problem is . . . not very different from the problems of
changing the smoking habits of the American public. Pres-
ently we know that smoking is dangerous to health. Despite this knowledge, many people are unable to change
their smoking habits, and many others take up this harmful habit. The task of changing smoking habits is probably
more formidable than changing the reading practices of
school systems. . . . With the recognition by taxpayers
and educators alike that the school must be accountable
in some sense for the products of its system, we may well
be moving toward an era in which schools will be doing
a more efficient job of teaching reading.

And Dr. Barbara Bateman of the University of Oregon says
flatly:

Near failure-proof methods for teaching all children to
read are already available. Continued failure of schools
to employ these [phonics-first] programs is at best negli-
gent and at worst malicious.

4

The Great Coverup

To stay in business despite the mounting research evidence and the near-unanimous opinions of leading scientists, the look-and-say educators had to conduct a vigilant and ceaseless coverup campaign.

For over fifty years, whenever a new exposure of their ancient gimmick threatened, someone—usually a professor on the payroll of a look-and-say textbook publisher—was sent into the breach to defend the system. This has been going on year after year, until today even some of the best minds in the field are confused or uninformed about certain areas of their own profession.

It's impossible to trace, incident by incident, the history of this gigantic coverup. In this chapter I'll simply give some of the highlights. I'll begin in 1928, with Professor Arthur I. Gates.

Professor Gates, of Teachers College, Columbia University, was then at the point of starting the Macmillan look-and-say series. But there were those studies clearly showing that look-and-say was inferior to phonics. What to do? Professor Gates hit upon the ingenious idea of "intrinsic" phonics. He'd start first graders on look-and-say, then at the end of first grade give them a little bit of phonics and run some tests to show that with this added ingredient look-and-say came out ahead.

He tested children in four New York City first-grade classrooms. Lo and behold, at the end of the year the children who'd had "intrinsic" phonics came out with better comprehension scores than those who had started with systematic phonics first. In his book *Methods in Primary Reading* (1928) Gates proudly announced this result to the world. The way was open to drive phonics-first out of American schools.

When I came upon Gates's results in my research for *Why*

Johnny Can't Read, I wondered how he'd done it. After all, by 1955 there were eleven studies that came out the other way. I studied the Gates data and found that Gates's tests had all been timed, which gave the quick-guessing look-and-say kids a clear advantage over the accurate but slower phonics-first readers. Also, the teachers of "intrinsic" or "incidental" phonics obviously treated the phonics instruction as anything *but* incidental. On the contrary, they did all they could to make Professor Gates's experiment come out the way he wanted.

Twelve years after I wrote my book, Dr. Jeanne Chall's *Learning to Read: The Great Debate* came out. Dr. Chall was in full agreement with what I'd said about Gates. The tests were timed, she wrote, which was unfair to the phonics-first kids, and the teachers *had* paid special attention to the teaching of "incidental" phonics. In a footnote on page 112 of her book she quoted "recent correspondence" with Professor Gates: "His intrinsic-phonics materials were extremely well programmed, teaching the alphabet along with the words. Thus, both groups probably received similar amounts of decoding practice."

In other words, forty years after the event, Professor Gates admitted he'd manipulated the experiment.

Let's go on to another major event in the Great Coverup. In 1955 my book *Why Johnny Can't Read* became a national best-seller. The educational journals answered in full cry, attacking me as an ignoramus, a propagandist—they never said for whom or what—a crank, a menace to the cause of good education. In December 1955, half a year after the publication of my book, *The Reading Teacher* came out with a special issue on phonics. It was filled with anti-Flesch outbursts, including a lengthy piece elaborately analyzing the propaganda techniques I had supposedly used in my book.

As to the eleven scientific studies I had reviewed, old Professor William S. Gray, senior author of the Dick-and-Jane, Scott, Foresman look-and-say readers, was called back from retirement to rebut my data. His answer was rather feeble. He never said that my account of the eleven studies was wrong or distorted. All he had to offer in reply was a study by Buswell published in 1922 and a study of his own, which he'd done in 1915 when he was in his twenties.

I read the Buswell study and found that it was a study of

eye movements, which offered no statistical data whatever. "The present investigation," Dr. Buswell wrote, "does not yield the type of data necessary for a judgment of methods, and consequently no attempt has been made to evaluate them."

It's true that Professor Gray's forty-year-old experiment compared the then widely used Aldine method, which was look-and-say, with the long-forgotten Ward method, which offered somewhat diluted phonics. And what did Professor Gray find when he tested those third graders long ago? "There was practically no difference in the average scores."

Let me go on to the next devastating review of phonics vs. look-and-say research, the one by Gurren and Hughes in 1965. How did the look-and-say forces answer that one? By utter silence. One article in an educational journal wasn't worth rolling out the big guns.

When the book *Learning to Read: The Great Debate* by Dr. Jeanne Chall came out in 1967, it couldn't be dealt with as easily. The research evidence was too massive and too detailed. So the look-and-say educators did the next best thing: they reviewed the book to death. There was an orgy of nitpicking, making it seem that Dr. Chall's monumental work was flawed, partly wrong, still controversial and unproven.

I checked through most of the two dozen reading-instruction textbooks—the books used in teachers' college courses to teach future reading teachers how to do their job. Typically, they mentioned Dr. Chall's book, but immediately proceeded to put it in a dubious light. For instance, *Reading in the Elementary School* by George D. and Evelyn B. Spache (fourth edition, 1977) gives Chall's book a brief paragraph and then says, "Many reviewers of this book did not feel that Chall had proved her theory, particularly when she depended so strongly upon studies over a long period of time from a wide variety of sources which often differ in their instructional practices from Chall's definition." (As you see, Dr. Chall's thoroughness is neatly used as a weapon against her.)

Or take another example. The book *Reading Instruction: Diagnostic Teaching in the Classroom* by Larry Harris and Carl B. Smith (second edition, 1976) also gives Chall's book a paragraph and follows it up with the sentence "The research evidence is not strong enough to convince every reading authority that intensive decoding is the way to begin instruction in reading."

The latest reading instruction textbook is *Developmental Reading: A Psycholinguistic Perspective* by Daniel R. Hittleman (1978). As you can see from the title, Hittleman is a follower of Frank Smith and Kenneth and Yetta Goodman. What does he have to say about Chall's book? Nothing at all. Neither the book nor "the Great Debate" is mentioned. As to phonics-first or decoding, there's a brief explanation of why it is useless.

In spite of all this, Professor Chall's book had some effect. In the years after it appeared, the look-and-say publishers decided that the Great Coverup had to be intensified and injected increasing amounts of token phonic window dressing into their basal readers. In 1977 they were rewarded for their efforts by a brochure written by Professor Chall, entitled *Reading 1967–1977: A Decade of Change and Promise*. It contained the following two sentences:

> By the middle 1970s most of the published beginning reading programs had a code emphasis (Popp, 1975). Even those that were classified as meaning emphasis had earlier and heavier decoding programs in the first grade—an emphasis on phonics found only in the strongest code-emphasis programs of the early 1960s.

Houghton Mifflin and Ginn & Company were quick to quote these two sentences in their sales materials and have used them to sell more of their look-and-say basal readers.

Since this quotation from Professor Chall plays a large part in the present phase of the Great Coverup, let's look at it a little more closely. The first sentence, saying that "most of the published beginning reading programs had a code emphasis" is plainly wrong. I checked the reference to Dr. Helen M. Popp's 1975 article, "Current Practices in the Teaching of Beginning Reading." It says no such thing.

The second sentence is trickier. It says that basal readers "classified as meaning emphasis"—that is, look-and-say readers—had "an emphasis on phonics found only in the strongest code-emphasis programs of the early 1960s." What does that mean? It does *not* mean that the phonics content in the look-and-say readers now matches that of the phonics-first readers.

It says only that the phonics you now find in the look-and-say basals is "found only" in the phonics-first readers of the early 1960s.

Now if you stay with me for another minute, I'll explain what this really means. In the early 1960s, there were just a few phonics-first programs, like Economy, Lippincott, and Open Court. By definition they taught *all* of phonics right at the start. The look-and-say readers in those days had virtually no phonics—maybe a smidgen of 1 percent or less.

After 1967, Houghton Mifflin, Ginn, and the rest, spurred by Professor Chall's book, put in more phonics. How much? Professor William K. Durr, senior author of the Houghton Mifflin series, obligingly explained in a letter:

> Houghton Mifflin is not a look-and-say series and has, in fact, been a phonics-first program for many years. The facts, easily verified by an examination of the *Houghton Mifflin Reading Series,* show that children are taught the twenty-two most consistent and reliable phonic elements (*b, c, d, f, g, h, j, k, l, m, n, p, r, s, t, v, w, y, ch, sh, th,* and *wh*) before they begin to read stories in their first pre-primer. The facts are that children are taught a decoding technique that uses these letter-sounds together with an understanding of the meaning of the material being read.

What percentage of phonics does this amount to? The reading instruction textbook *Teaching Reading* by Walcutt, Lamport, and McCracken contains a phonic inventory, listing all the items normally taught to children in a phonics-first series as they learn to read. The inventory adds up to 181 items, including all the letters and sounds plus such spelling patterns as *ng, scr, oi, ight,* etc.

If the 100 percent figure is 181, then the 22 phonic elements taught by Houghton Mifflin amount to 12 percent. Most other look-and-say series offer even less.

So it turns out that the vaunted switch to phonics after the publication of Professor Chall's book has brought an increase of token phonics window dressing from less than 1 percent to about 12 percent. This is still a small fraction of the total phonics children must be taught at the start in order to become fluent readers. And it doesn't take into account the fact that those look-and-say first graders are being trained to guess words from context, and are *never* told about the secret alphabetic code.

I hope this explains the true meaning of Professor Chall's two sentences and their place in the scheme of the Great Coverup.

Let's go back to the research review by Dr. Dykstra in 1973. His main added evidence was the U.S. Office of Education study of twenty-seven first-grade programs, of which he was the director. Dykstra's report pointed out that phonics-first, particularly the Lippincott readers, had won a complete victory. The look-and-say educators concealed and misrepresented these findings. In an editorial in the October 1966 *Reading Teacher*, Dr. Russell Stauffer, senior author of the Holt, Rinehart & Winston look-and-say readers, wrote:

> There is no one method of teaching reading. . . . Every method described used words, and phonics, and pictures, and comprehension, and teachers. . . . There was no one phonic method that was pure. . . . And where does all this leave us? All the maligning that reading instruction has endured for the past decade has not led to the golden era. No approach has overcome individual differences or eliminated reading failure. . . . Now that we have slashed around wildly in the mire of accusations let us remember that reading without comprehension is not reading.

Eleven years later, in 1977, Dr. Dykstra reported sadly:

> Many of my colleagues in the field of reading have made and continue to make misleading and inaccurate statements concerning the major conclusions of the first-grade studies. . . . The popular view among professionals in the field of reading is that the first-grade studies found the teacher to be the most important variable in beginning reading instruction. . . . We came to no such conclusion. . . .
> We found that programs *did* differ in effectiveness. . . .

Children who learned to read in instructional programs emphasizing early and intensive teaching of phonetics demonstrated superior ability.

Dr. Dykstra has corrected misstatements about the outcome of the twenty-seven first-grade studies many times and in many places. But he has never caught up with the solid mass of commonly accepted untruths. To this day, almost all educators firmly believe that the twenty-seven studies showed that the teacher made the most important difference in how children learned to read and that no method proved to be superior.

Finally, we come to the monumental Follow Through project of the mid-seventies—programs for ex-Head Start children. That time it was the Distar phonics method that ran away with all honors. The Ford Foundation financed a thirty-three-page critique by a team of four researchers that appeared in a special issue of the *Harvard Educational Review* in the summer of 1978. Faulting the report on Follow Through on a dozen or more technical points, the team concluded that Distar's victory was spurious.

The outcome measures [they wrote], strongly favor models that concentrate on teaching mechanical skills. . . . Follow Through was to be an investigation of models of comprehensive early childhood education—not just reading, not just arithmetic, not just language usage. . . . Although who did best on the Metropolitan Achievement Test [of reading and math] might be a valid question, it would be wrong to confuse that question with the one that was actually asked.

In other words, now that Distar showed up strongest in all the achievement tests, let's pretend that wasn't the point of the studies.

This was answered by three U.S. Office of Education experts who had supervised the project. "Compensatory education can work," they wrote. ". . . Though not successful everywhere and not uniformly successful in all its outcomes, that model [Distar] showed the best pattern of success."

And that's where the matter stands now. After almost seventy years of research, after 124 studies leaving look-and-say without a shred of scientific respectability, it is still used in 85 percent of our classrooms, poisoning the minds and crippling the educational growth of tens of millions of children. The federal government, carrying out its Congressional mandate, has poured billions of dollars into the twenty-seven cooperative first-grade studies and compensatory education projects like Head Start and Follow Through. Those projects proved without any doubt that phonics-first is superior to look-and-say.

The educators have ignored this mountain of solid evidence and continued their programmed retardation in our schools.

How did they do it? Mainly by turning the competition for textbook sales to the schools into an annual beauty contest. Almost every other year, each of the competitors comes out with "new, improved" models, renamed, refurbished, and, if possible, newly and more gaudily illustrated. There's no other country in the world where children learn to read from such handsome books.

Does that improve their reading skill? It wasn't until 1967 that a researcher, Dr. S. Jay Samuels, got curious as to the answer to that question.

It turned out that pictures not only don't help kids to learn whole words by look-and-say, but are an actual hindrance. Somewhat surprised, Dr. Samuels repeated his original experiment in another, more classroomlike setting. The result was the same. The simple truth was that a child, when confronted by a word and a picture, will look at the picture *first*. The more attractive the picture, the more it will interfere with word learning.

After Samuels's innovative research, nineteen—yes, nineteen—more researchers followed in his footsteps. Eventually Samuels summarized the whole series of studies in an article in the *Review of Educational Research*.

Dr. Samuels's summary was devastating. He wrote:

1. The bulk of the research findings on the effect of pictures on acquisition of a sight-vocabulary was that pictures interfere with learning to read.
2. There was almost unanimous agreement that pictures when used as adjuncts to the printed text, do not facilitate comprehension.

5

The Ten Alibis

The first chapter of this book was published, slightly cut, as an article in *Family Circle* magazine (November 1, 1979). It brought thousands of letters.

Most of them were from mothers, thanking me for writing the piece and telling tales of woe of how their children were miseducated at school and how they were given the brushoff when they complained.

The letters from educators were sharply different. They were full of personal abuse. They called me "a liar," "grossly misinformed," "dastardly," "criminal," "libelous," "alarmist," a "demagogue," a user of "scare tactics" and "half-truths." They said the magazine was doing a great disservice to its readers by printing the article. They said I knew nothing about children, about education, about the English language. They said I was "simplistic" and "absurd."

One reading teacher wrote it was "a negative article that was unnecessarily distressful to parents and inciteful to educators."

A school principal took the magazine to task for printing such an "irresponsible" article. He said it "was filled with misinformation, which, unfortunately, some parents will believe."

A university professor wrote to the editor he "was amazed that you would condone, indeed even permit such 'factual' junk to sully your pages."

A reading coordinator wrote the magazine had "reduced its standards by publishing a fact-distorted attention-getter."

And so on and on and on. The educators were "shocked," "disturbed," "infuriated." One of them summed it all up by saying that the article was a "pedogogical trough of swill."

In short, the look-and-say educators' letters were prize examples of the aggressive tactics they have used for fifty years.

This doesn't mean their letters didn't offer any arguments. They were full of them. All the old standbys were trotted out—the old, old alibis that have been used to defend look-and-say ever since it was first shown up as phony seventy years ago.

I went through the whole stack of letters and sorted out the ten favorite alibis. They were:

1. "Everything Is Hunky-Dory"
2. "We Do Teach Phonics"
3. "No One Method Is Best"
4. "English Isn't Phonetic"
5. "Word Calling Isn't Reading"
6. "Your Child Isn't Ready"
7. "Your Child Is Disabled"
8. "It's the Parents' Fault"
9. "Too Much TV"
10. "We Now Teach *All* Children"

Let me explain briefly exactly what each of these slogans means.

Alibi No. 1 *"Everything is hunky-dory."*

As everybody in the country knows by now, the statistics on illiteracy and declining reading achievement are appalling. Every few months there is another front-page story about a new batch of statistics or scientific data. It is common knowledge that millions of children and grownups can't read, write, or spell.

But if you're an educator, this is all propaganda, made up by critics of the schools. American schools, they insist, are doing fine—just fine.

One of them writes, "I believe if you canvass the schools across America you would find that with the advent of reading assessments, state and national funding, use of libraries, and a heavy emphasis on how reading should be taught in the schools, one would find students are better readers than ever before."

Another one writes, "Children not only read better but are doing so at a younger age."

And a reading consultant says proudly, "Historically and statistically, our students *are* reading better than ever!" (The italics and the exclamation point are hers.)

They sound so convinced they clearly have fallen for their own propaganda. In Chapter 6 I'll tell exactly what the statistics show and how they were juggled in the educational journals and public statements.

Alibi No. 2 *"We do teach phonics."*

As I showed in Chapter 1—with plenty of examples—there's an astronomical difference between the real phonics-first series and the window-dressing token phonics being offered in the look-and-say readers. To be shown up like this makes the educators particularly mad. For decades they've been trying to bamboozle the public and pretend they teach phonics. And here I am again accusing them of using old, discredited look-and-say. Heavens no, perish the thought. They're "eclectic," they use all methods combined, they give each child all the phonics he or she should know.

A reading teacher writes, "I am using one of your 'dirty dozen' . . . and it is anything but a look-and-say series."

Another: "Your categorization of certain publishers as 'look-and-say' publishers is totally unfounded. In fact the major reading series on your 'look-and-say' list have been strong proponents of increased instruction in phonics."

A third: "Half the curriculums on the list under the 'Dismal Dozen' do utilize a synthetic approach to the teaching of reading (phonics-first)."

They've apparently been completely taken in by the salestalk of the look-and-say publishers. A good many of them, of course, have never seen any of the good phonics-first series and have no way of knowing how bad the look-and-say readers really are. More on all this in Chapter 7.

Alibi No. 3 *"No one method is best."*

This alibi says, in essence, that anyone who says reading should be taught with phonics is a nut—a crank who peddles phony patent medicine or a panacea. We, the educators, know best and teach our children with a carefully designed mixture of all available methods, fine-tuned to give each child what's best for him or her. Those phonics nuts are just ignoramuses who think one method is the answer to all the complexities of the reading problem.

This alibi has it all upside down. It's the look-and-say method—Gedike's old gimmick—that's peddled as a panacea and the phonics method that's based on common sense and scientific research. It matches the nature of the subject. If you teach typing, you familiarize the student with the keyboard; if you teach driving, you tell him or her how the gears work; if you teach cooking, you start with a few basic recipes. You don't tell students to just go ahead and type, or drive, or cook. In the same way, you start to teach reading by teaching what sounds the letters stand for.

But the educators don't see it that way. A teacher writes, "All of us are individuals, and we learn in different ways. To assume that one way of teaching is the answer for all ignores this very important fact. Simple answers to complex problems very seldom, if ever, exist."

A principal echoes this: "There is no 'one way' or 'best way' to teach reading to all children. To suggest such a panacea is to display a certain innocence and naïveté about the hard realities of teaching all of the children of all the people to read."

"Only a person who has never taught reading," another teacher writes, "would say that all children should learn to read by the 'phonics-first' approach. Children have different learning styles. A competent reading teacher will match a reading approach to the individual student."

A principal says, "There are as many learning styles as there are children. A teacher uses 'many' methods to meet these individual needs. If a child is an auditory learner then a phonics approach may work very well for him. If he is a visual learner, then he needs many materials he can 'see,' and 'look and say' may have a place in the construction of a curriculum for him."

Finally, here is an outburst from still another teacher: *"There is no 'best' way* to teach reading in our schools for one simple reason—CHILDREN DO NOT ALL LEARN THE SAME WAY!"

I'll have more to say about all this and about the myth of "the auditory and the visual child" in Chapter 8.

Alibi No. 4 "English isn't phonetic."

Another old, old standby. You can't teach children by phonics because English isn't phonetic. Actually, as I'll show later, English writing is 97.4 percent phonetic and decodable, but the educators have never looked at the research that proves this. To them, English is just like Chinese—you have to teach it word by word.

"The English language," a teacher writes, "is not phonetically regular. For practically every rule, there are exceptions."

And Ginn & Company, one of the look-and-say publishers, came out with a defensive "fact sheet" containing this gem: "Mr. Flesch paints an unrealistic picture of the English language. While the [Ginn & Company] basal reader has words in it which are approximately 80 percent decodable by a phonics process, the real world language is not as regular. Therefore, care must be taken to teach children to decode words in other ways than phonics first so that they have other strategies to use when phonics fails them."

This sounds as if the Ginn & Company basal reader series taught phonics first and look-and-say only later, as an emergency strategy in those unfortunate cases when phonics doesn't work. One look at their materials shows that nothing could be further from the truth.

Alibi No. 5 "Word calling isn't reading."

To understand this, you have to know what educators mean by "word calling." Ever since look-and-say was invented, they've insisted that phonics-trained readers don't understand what they read. When a phonics-trained child reads a word like *cat*, he pronounces the sounds, they say, but has no idea what kind of animal is meant. Children have to be taught meanings; they must understand, they must comprehend. Otherwise what they do can't be called reading. They're not readers but word callers.

This is so ridiculous that it's hard to discuss it with a straight face. *Of course* a child will understand a word that's in his speaking and listening vocabulary, when he reads it off the page. But he has to get it off the page first, by pronouncing the letters, before he can apply his knowledge of vocabulary.

This simple truth should be obvious to everyone, but it isn't to thousands of people in the American educational Establishment. Listen to them:

A principal: "Lacking a basic definition of reading, you confuse reading with recognizing words."

A teacher: "Reading is much more than being able to break down a word phonetically. Reading is comprehending the printed words. Reading tests understanding."

Another teacher: "You seem to consider the ability to pronounce words properly to be reading. Reading is comprehension—understanding! Without it there is no reading; there is only word calling. This may be a useful skill for showing off six year olds to relatives but of little value to tomorrow's doctors and lawyers. For a person to be able to pronounce 'poisonous—not to be taken internally' may make him sound educated but to understand those words could save his life!"

A school superintendent writes: "You say that 'reading means getting meaning from certain combinations of letters. Teach the child what each letter stands for and he can read.' Sounds reasonable? Read the following: 'The autochthonous hominid was imperturbable.' I am certain you were able to translate the sequence of letters into sounds, but did you derive any meaning from the process? Your approach to reading omits the most critical part of the entire reading process—meaning. Parents should not be as concerned with *how* their children are being taught but rather with whether they are being taught to read for meaning, for enjoyment, for a broadening of their horizons."

A reading specialist and Title I instructor writes: "You say that children who have been taught to read via phonics can read anything presented. This absolutely is untrue. What you mean is that children can pronounce/sound out/decode (they all mean the same) but this is not, I repeat, *is not* reading. I can just see parents reading the article and believing their offspring can read when they are in reality just sounding out words. In the reading business, we call that word calling. In order to say that reading is taking place, comprehension must, absolutely must, take place. So a child can pronounce words like *catastrophe* or any word in the dictionary, reading simply is not taking place without comprehension."

This is not only ungrammatical, it's incoherent. *Of course* a phonics-trained first grader will be able to read *catastrophe* off the page, but he probably won't know what it means. The point is that a look-and-say-trained child won't be able to read the word *catastrophe at all.* Maybe, when he's in senior high school, he'll be able to figure it out from the first two letters *c* and *a* and from the context—*if* he's learned by then the meaning of the word, and *if* he doesn't wildly guess *calamity,* or *caterpillar,* or *cafeteria,* or whatnot, and *if* he doesn't simply skip the word and read on.

It's hard to decide which of the ten alibis is the most ludicrous, but I've always felt that this one deserves the prize.

Alibi No. 6 "Your child isn't ready."

This alibi has to do with "reading readiness." It's so simple: if a child is still in first or second grade and the mother complains he can't read, you just say the child isn't ready yet. No fuss, no bother—just an easy stall. Next year, when the child still can't read, we'll think of something else.

My letter writers phrased this in dozens of different ways: "Why can't Johnny read?" one of them wrote. "There are a multitude of answers to this question. As a first grade teacher I see many children who are just plain not ready yet. There is no magic age at which all children are mature enough to start the difficult task of learning to read. Yet children are sent off to first grade at age six. 'Ready or not here I come.' Children should be evaluated before beginning school to determine if they are ready. In this way the child would not be doomed to fail first, second or third grade."

Another teacher echoes this: "Not all children are ready to begin reading at the age of six. For reasons too numerous to mention, the child may not have the necessary background of experience necessary for the successful beginning reader."

A reading specialist tops this by the following sentence about the look-and-say-trained illiterate junior high school students I'd mentioned in my article: "The paragraph about the Houghton Mifflin series and its attempts to improve the reading of late bloomers is carping to the point of being amusing."

Junior high school students? Late bloomers indeed!

Alibi No. 7 "Your child is disabled."

The easiest thing to do with a child who can't read is to put him into a special education class. In the past twenty or thirty years, our schools have labeled hundreds of thousands of children "dyslexic," "minimally brain-damaged," "learning disabled," or what have you. They didn't learn to read by whatever standard was used, *therefore* there was something wrong with them and they had to be put into separate classes. By now, the federal government has shelled out billions of dollars for this procedure, and millions of children have been made miserable, and their parents worried and scared.

I don't mean to say that there are no children with organic disorders, but they are few and far between. The vast majority of those unhappy, stigmatized children are simply the victims of look-and-say.

But the educators would never accept this. One of them writes, with the full authority of the expert, "Children sometimes experience undiagnosed hearing or vision problems which interfere with reading instruction. Children with learning difficulties should obviously be examined by a doctor to determine the presence or absence of any underlying medical problems."

I will say more about this tragedy in Chapter 12.

Alibi No. 8 "It's the parents' fault."

Of course the educators don't usually say this out loud, but their meaning is unmistakable. It's never the school that's at fault; it's the home. Here are some samples:

A remedial reading teacher: "If all parents were willing to work as hard to teach their children as you suggest, most of our children would not have reading problems to begin with. My years as a remedial reading teacher have convinced me that our best readers come from homes rich in reading materials, reading experiences, and *reading* parents (parents who read to and with children as well as for their own enjoyment). In the final analysis, the only reading program that can work 100 percent of the time with 100 percent of our children is the one started in the home and built upon by the educators."

Another teacher: "Open indifference to a child's reading

progress by one or both parents often triggers a similar indifference to reading by the child. More serious problems are caused when the child experiences the effects of conflicts between parents, parental neglect, or parental abuse. Damage caused by these problems entails more than reading ability and correction of these conditions often requires professional help."

Another: "Other problems that interfere with the child's desire to learn to read include such things as divorce, television, or both parents work, so no one has time to read to Johnny or listen to him read. The list of reasons goes on and on."

As you see, this last little package of alibis includes TV. Which brings us to

Alibi No. 9 *"Too much TV."*

The idea is that children don't get the reading habit or do any homework because they sit in front of the TV set all the time. Never mind the obvious fact that they can't read any words beyond the measly 1,500 they're taught at school. *Of course* they don't read books, for the simple reason that they haven't been taught how. But TV is such a handy scapegoat the educators never fail to mention it. "There is research to prove," one of them assures me, "that limiting television watching helps a great deal." (See Chapter 14.)

Alibi No. 10 *"We now teach* all *children."*

With great pride and conviction the educators say that America, the citadel of democracy, is the only country in the world that has taken on the job of giving each child an education. Aren't we wonderful? We try to teach all children to read—in contrast to other, less enlightened countries. So, naturally, some of those children are not educable—if the truth were known they are the dregs of society, not capable of receiving the boon of education we bestow on them.

For instance, one reading expert writes, "Do you realize a much larger percentage of our students go on to college than did a number of years ago? Do you also realize that our country is one of the few in the world who attempt to teach *every* child to read?"

Another educator puts it this way, "While there are admittedly some things wrong with our educational system today—there certainly are many things that are right. Nowhere else

in the world, except Canada, is *everyone* given an equal opportunity to attend school at any level."

An elementary schoolteacher just uses the common cliché:
"The American educational system tries to reach all children."

Finally, there's a reading teacher who comes right out with
it: "Classroom teachers and reading specialists teach children
with innumerable combinations of genetic factors and exper-
iential backgrounds."

You see the little word *genetic?* There it is, black on white.
Alibi No. 10, whichever way it is put, is always racist. Children
who don't do well in reading are impervious to all the wonderful educational opportunities we offer them. Why? Because
they're black, Chicano, or just simply poor—the sons and
daughters of lowborn riffraff who are too dumb to learn how
to read.

I'll say more about this ultimate alibi in Chapter 15. Meanwhile I'll wind up this bundle of quotations with the official
statement issued by the 65,000-member International Reading
Association, representing the quarter-billion-dollar look-and-
say business. Three weeks after my *Family Circle* article appeared, the board of directors of the association adopted a
"position statement." Haughtily, they didn't mention my name.

In light of recent public statements that suggest that
reading can best be taught by using a single method
through strong emphasis on a specific skill or through
the use of a specific set of materials, the Board of Directors
of the International Reading Association emphasizes that
learning to read is a complex process requiring not only
the ability to recognize words, but also the ability to comprehend and evaluate the meaning of written materials.
The most important factor related to success in learning
to read is the teacher. Differences in the learning styles
and abilities of children emphasize the need for a variety
of approaches to meet those individual needs. No single
method or approach nor any one set of instructional materials has been proven to be most effective for all children.
Furthermore, to learn to read well, children must read
a substantial amount of material for useful purposes both
in school and at home.

Therefore, it is resolved that the Board of Directors

of the International Reading Association recommends that parents and teachers exercise caution and judgment when considering statements or selecting materials that advocate any single method or set of materials as being the best one for teaching reading. Moreover, the Board expresses concern about those who use scare tactics and oversimplification to support their own easy solutions for teaching children to read.

The board of directors showed admirable restraint. They used only three of the ten standard alibis—numbers 3, 5 and 8.

To end this chapter, let me quote three letters that gave me pleasure:

The first said, "We have a daughter in grade one, so found this article very interesting and informative as we have the Ginn series in our schools. . . . I showed her the word *jam* and she looked at it and immediately said *jump,* so now we are doing phonics every day and she has stopped guessing and has found it very interesting and fun. We are still working on the A E I O U and when she wants to know bigger words that are on a package or something, I show how it can be broken down and sounded out and she usually comes up with the word."

The second letter said, "I have been using your original book to help an eight-year-old girl with her reading for the past five months. She has progressed from 'scholastically retarded' to excellent reading at grade 3 level, so thank you from both of us."

The third letter said, "Thank you so much for your article. My son has been struggling for seven years with his reading. I now understand why! I've been working with him for three weeks with intensive phonics—and he's improved 100 percent. Thanks again and keep it up."

6

"Everything Is Hunky-Dory"

On February 13, 1979, Dr. Harold Howe II, Vice President for Education and Research of the Ford Foundation and former U.S. Commissioner of Education, appeared before the U.S. Senate Subcommittee on Education, Arts and Humanities to testify on the teaching and learning of basic academic skills in schools. He started his testimony with the following statement: "The significance of the much reported decline of learning in American schools is exaggerated and is not as serious a matter as the popularization of it suggests."

This is the most high-sounding version I've seen so far of the old standby Alibi No. 1—"Everything is hunky-dory."

There is no need in this book to give you a lot of statistics to prove what's happening. Like every other American, you know that our educational system is in very bad shape and that we have a lot of illiterates in this country.

What most people *don't* know is how staggering the figures really are. Before I started this book, I made it my business to find the exact size of the problem.

There are no official statistics, I learned, but the nearest thing to them is the data that came out of the Adult Performance Level study (APL), which was done at the University of Texas in 1975. A recent survey, *Adult Illiteracy in the United States* (1979), sponsored by the Ford Foundation, also refers to that APL study as a basic source.

I asked the University of Texas to send me the report and the questionnaire that was used. Here's what I found:

The APL statistics were based on the findings of interviews with 7,500 U.S. adults, conducted nationwide. Each interview lasted about an hour. The house-to-house survey was done by

59

the Opinion Research Center of Princeton, New Jersey, a well-known polling firm.

The questionnaire consisted of forty items, dealing with what the researchers called "functional competency"—the sum total of competencies important to success as adults. One of those competencies, of course, is the ability to read.

It was found that 21.7 percent of U.S. adults between 18 and 65 couldn't correctly answer such questions as these:

> If the label on a medicine bottle says, "Take 2 pills twice a day," how many pills should you take in 1 day?

> A government brochure about termites says, "No matter what protective measures you take, periodic inspection should be made at least every six months if you live where termites are common." You live in such an area. How often should you have your house inspected?

I studied all the other items in the questionnaire and found that they were just as clearcut. Obviously, a person who can't answer such simple questions is functionally illiterate. Webster's *New Collegiate Dictionary* (1973) defines a functional illiterate as "a person having had some schooling but not meeting a minimum standard of literacy."

As I said, the APL report said that 21.7 percent of U.S. adults between 18 and 65 fell into that category. This meant 23 million people.

This number is a sweeping indictment of the U.S. school system and the reading instruction method used in most schools. According to the APL data, 19 million of those 23 million have had at least four years of schooling. Virtually all of them were taught reading by the look-and-say method. How can this enormous failure possibly be defended?

The chief defender among the educators, the man who has made it his life's work to prove that "everything is hunky-dory," is Professor Roger B. Farr of Indiana University, senior author of the Laidlaw Brothers look-and-say readers. In his article, "Is Johnny's/Mary's Reading Getting Worse?," which appeared in the April 1977 issue of the magazine *Educational Leadership*, he wrote, "If we are concerned about national 'basic literacy,' we can forge ahead seeking improvement confident that we are doing quite well."

How did he reach that conclusion in the face of the crushing facts uncovered by the APL and other studies?

The number-one statistical "proof" used by Professor Farr in his article—and also when he appeared before the Senate subcommittee I mentioned earlier—is the National Assessment of Educational Progress survey, published in 1976.

Here's the story behind that survey. In the early 1970s, when the public clamor about American education got louder and louder, the look-and-say educators—that is, the Education Commission of the United States—with $40 million in private and federal funds, set up the National Assessment of Educational Progress in Denver, Colorado. The NAEP collected educational statistics on school achievement in the 1970–1971 academic year. Four years later, in 1974–1975 it repeated the process. Then, on September 21, 1976, it published a press release. It bore the following headline:

It's a Fact—Johnny, Age 9, Is Reading Better

The first paragraph said, "Who says Johnny—and Mary—can't read? Contrary to popular opinion, Johnny and Mary, at age 9 at least, are reading better than their counterparts of a few years ago."

That sounded fine, except for the awkward fact that it was totally misleading. Dr. Richard L. Venezky wrote in the April 1977 *Reading Teacher* that the NAEP press release and report were "inexcusable."

What did the report actually say? It said that three age groups of students had been retested after the four-year interval—nine-year-olds, thirteen-year-olds, and seventeen-year-olds. There were a number of different tests, one of which was reading comprehension. The nine-year-olds, in this *one* test, did better in 1975 than in 1971. They answered on the average 65 percent of the questions correctly. In 1971 they'd gotten only 64 percent right. At the other two age levels and in all other categories there was no progress, and in some cases there was some further decline.

Why did those nine-year-olds make their 1 percent progress over four years? Professor Farr's article gives us a clue. He says progress in the lower grades is "almost certainly due to federally funded supplementary reading programs"—which means the recent slight inroads of phonics-first.

Instead of focusing on the 1 percent progress of *one* group in *one* category, let's look at what the NAEP survey actually shows. It says, in plain English, that in 1975, 35 percent of the nation's fourth graders *could not read.* Of the eighth graders, 37 percent *could not read.* Of the twelfth graders, 23 percent *could not read.*

What does "could not read" mean? It means that they couldn't answer correctly such items as this one: "The label on a cat food can says 'Until they reach three months old, feed kittens Meow-Wow Dinner about every four hours. Let them eat all they want.' How should you feed a two-month-old kitten?"

Please note that the test was given only to students *in school.* It didn't cover children *not* in school, that is, dropouts. (According to the *New York Times* of October 17, 1979, the New York City Board of Education officially estimated the high school dropout rate at 45 percent.) Which means that the percentage of functionally illiterates among high school seniors and other seventeen-year-olds was maybe as much as 40 percent or more—far higher than the adult illiteracy rate reported by the University of Texas APL study. Clearly the U.S. literacy rate, now down to that of Burma and Albania, will drop even lower.

And what did Professor Farr have to say to all that? He was head of the NAEP evaluation panel. He wrote, "I think all ages are doing exceptionally well on the items that are straightforward, basic, literal." Most of his colleagues on the evaluating panel were associated with the Ginn & Company look-and-say series. One of them, Professor William Blanton, was even more enthusiastic than Farr. He wrote, "Performance on the functional literacy items, items that involve activities like reading a telephone bill or following the directions on a container of cat food, is so high that it does challenge a lot of what has been said in the last few years. Seventeen-year-olds are definitely doing well—better than previously—on these kinds of items."

Let me repeat: Among *high school seniors* attending school, 23 percent could not read simple directions. Specifically, 21 percent flunked the cat food item. And this catastrophic result is what Professor William Blanton of Ginn & Company proudly announced to the world as a sign of progress!

But all this—about one quarter of the nation sinking into illiteracy—is just the tip of the iceberg. A mountainous tip, but still a *tip*. Underneath are all those millions, students and adults, who can read but just barely. Look-and-say training has enabled them to work their way slowly through a piece of simple prose and understand it after a fashion, but that's about all. They've never developed the skill of fluent reading. Their reading is slow, halting, and uncertain.

How many of those slow readers are there? Again the Adult Performance Level survey has an answer. According to their statistics—and remember, their findings were fully confirmed by the pro-Establishment National Assessment survey—in 1975 there were 32.2 percent U.S. adults who could read but were only just above the borderline. They could read a label on a medicine bottle or a want ad in the paper, but nothing more complicated. These 32.2 percent, in 1975, added up to 34 million people. They were "minimally proficient." Only the remaining 46.1 percent of the population between 18 and 65 were fully proficient and fluent readers. As you can see, *the illiterates plus the slow readers are now a majority of the U.S. population.*

How can you tell a slow reader from a fast one? In the *Journal of Learning Disabilities* for May 1972 a Canadian physician, Dr. Carl L. Kline, gave a good description:

A common prototype of reading disabilities seen in adolescents is the bright high school student who reads at or near grade level, but who has a spelling disability, is a slow reader, who misreads some words, omits words, substitutes words, and occasionally reverses (reads words from right to left instead of left to right). . . . In working with [those students] one must anticipate that there will be a residual spelling problem, even after the reading problem is largely overcome. Once the reading problem is alleviated, one is faced with a student who knows how to read, at last, but who doesn't know how to study. Having avoided reading for years because of the reading problem, a considerable gap often exists in terms of general knowledge, vocabulary and ability to scan material in order to pick out the important facts from an assignment.

The most obvious sign of a slow reader, brought up on look-and-say, is his or her bizarre spelling. As Dr. Kline says, even if such a student learns how to read fluently, he'll probably stay a poor speller all his life. In the November 1974 issue of the *Bulletin of the New York Academy of Medicine,* Dr. R. Arthur Gindin, Associate Professor of Neurosurgery at the Medical College of Georgia, writes of common spelling errors of freshmen in medical school. Here is a partial list of the misspellings he found in their papers:

accomidation	ecessive
amblitory	extention
analized	nausia
apperent	occassions
apethetic	occular
assending	occurance
bilatterally	refered
cinammon	subtrat
develope	tremmor

These millions of slow readers and bizarre spellers also account for the decline in recent years of the SAT (Scholastic Aptitude Test) scores. As I mentioned in the first chapter, the average scores on these college entrance tests have been steadily going down since 1963. The average on the verbal part of the test was 478 in 1963 and fell to 424 in 1980. Since the full range of scores is from 200 to 800, this means a 9 percent drop in seventeen years—an enormous decline in the verbal capacities of high school students who want to go to college. (Their math scores dropped almost as much.)

In 1977 a group of educators formed a twenty-one-member panel, chaired by Willard Wirtz, former U.S. Secretary of Labor, to study the reasons for this alarming decline. The panel found a number of possible reasons but couldn't pinpoint a

specific source of the trouble. It specifically *excluded* the post–
World War II influx of less-qualified applicants.

I am convinced that the main reason for the decline is the
look-and-say method. Let me explain why. According to the
Wirtz report, one of the typical vocabulary questions follows
this pattern:

> The question below consists of a word in capital letters,
> followed by five lettered words or phrases. Choose the
> word or phrase that is most nearly *opposite* in meaning
> to the word in capital letters. . . .
> RECTITUDE: (A) deliberation (B) laziness (C) prejudice
> (D) laxity of morals (E) weakness of intellect

The correct answer to this sample question is D. Only 23
percent of typical students making a score of 450 had the right
answer. *That's only 3 percent above the pure chance score of
20 percent.*

Now let me show you how a student's answer to this type
of question depends on how he was taught to read in first
grade. Suppose he was taught by the phonics-first method. If
so, he was taught the complete alphabetic code so he could
sound out any unfamiliar word he came across.

The word *rectitude* is a rather rare word. According to the
Thorndike-Lorge frequency list, it occurs about once in a million words of general reading matter.

Suppose our phonics-trained student comes across the word
for the first time while he is in fourth grade. He'll look at it,
silently sound it out, and decide from the hint of "correct"
that it must mean something like righteousness. He'll store
this tentative meaning in his memory. Next time he comes
upon *rectitude*—a year later, maybe—he recalls this stored
memory and confirms it in this new context. He does the same
thing the third, fourth, and fifth time he encounters the word,
until its meaning is fixed in his mind. Maybe he hears it spoken
or tries it out as an item in his own speaking vocabulary.

This, in essence, is how a phonics-trained child learns the
meaning of words and builds his vocabulary.

Now consider the look-and-say trained reader. The word *rectitude* is of course *not* among the 1,500 or 3,000 words he
learns to recognize by sight during his first three or four school

years. By the time he's in fourth grade, he's never seen the word in print.

Suppose he comes across the word while he's in the fourth or fifth grade. This is unlikely to occur in one of his school textbooks, since they've been carefully cleansed of all but the simplest words. But suppose he comes across *rectitude* else-where—*if* he does any reading beyond what he has to.

He looks at *rectitude* and does what he's been trained to do. He tries to guess its meaning from the context and the first letter *r*. Maybe he also uses the second letter *e* as the basis of his guess. He may come up with *reserve, reputation, resistance, religion, reticence, reluctance, regularity* or some other *re* word he knows. Or he may stop cold. He may decide that the word must be *reticence* or *reserve,* or *reluctance,* or he may simply skip it and go on. In any case, since he has no way of deciphering *rectitude,* he does *not* learn its meaning from this first encounter.

Next time he comes upon *rectitude* while he's, say, in fifth grade. He still doesn't know what it means and goes through the same futile approach he used the first time. The same happens whenever he sees *rectitude* again in his reading. (This won't be often, since a look-and-say trained reader avoids reading as much as he can.)

Finally, as a high school junior or senior, he takes the Scholastic Aptitude Test. One of the questions deals with the word *rectitude.* With his background of repeated guessing, he can't possibly tell whether it means the opposite of *prejudice* or *laziness.* So he guesses. Four times out of five, he guesses wrong.

I went into all this detail because I know from experience that people who were taught reading by phonics or have discovered the secret of the alphabetic code by themselves don't understand the reading habits of those who were taught by look-and-say. It's almost impossible for them to imagine the difficulties of someone who doesn't know the alphabetic code. Since you, as a reader of a serious nonfiction book, are probably among that minority of Americans who do know the code, I'll illustrate this important point by two case histories.

The first is a letter I got from a woman I'll call Karen Field. I'll reprint it here with all the original spelling errors (including my name):

November 23, 1979

Rudolf Flech
Harper & Row
10 E. 53rd Street
New York, N.Y. 10022

Attention Mr. Flech:

After reading your article in the November 1, 1979
Family Circle magazine, Why Johnny Still Can't Read
made me feel a little better about my self. For a while
I thought it was all my fault I couldn't read or spell better.
I would like to know if you could help me learn phonics
and how to break the words into syllables.

I am a 34 year old female. I graduated from high school
June 1963. I have always had problems in reading and
spelling. It all started in my early years of schooling. I
was one of the victim of look and say or sight reading
not by phonics or syllables. I remember, the childern in
my class all had books with pictures and words in them.
We could look at the pictures, for example an apple. The
teacher would tell us to remember the word apple because it had two P's in it. This meant every time I saw
a word with two P's in it, I thought it said apple.

As the years went by I had to study very hard and
longer periods of time then someone else because I had
to memorize the spelling of words to pass my test. When
I went to junior high school, I ask if I could take a special
reading course but the class was full. I was not alone my
girl friends had the same problem.

After graduting from high school, I still have spelling
and reading problems. Sometimes it has been very up
setting to me. I sometime don't understand my problem.
I can read the every day newspaper but get stuck on
spelling and reading of names. When I'm finished reading
an article in the newspaper and someone ask me to spell
a word I just read, I can't spell it. I guess I'm still trying
to memorize the words. I saw an ad in the newspaper
for a tutor for reading and spelling but when I called,
the lady only would teach childern.

I would like to get a better job but I feel very insecure because of my spelling and reading problem. I do not like to play any spelling games for fear I will not be able to spell the words. I keep telling myself that their are probably some people worse off then me. I guess you are wondering how I spelled some of the words in this letter. All I can say is Thank God for the Websters Dictionary.

I would appreciate it very much if you would please respond to my problem by sending me Free Information. Enclosed is a self address envelope with postage.

Very truly yours,
Karen Field

I leave it to you to find all the errors in spelling, grammar and usage. Please note that Miss Field is a high school graduate and has a job, although not a good one. She is obviously an intelligent woman. As Dr. Kline says in his article, even if she learns to read better by a program in phonics-first, she'll probably never be a good speller.

Remember that Miss Field and her fellow victims of look-and-say are now the majority of the U.S. adult population.

Now let's move to my second case history. This is an excerpt from an unpublished article by Mrs. Margaret Bishop, who runs a reading tutoring program for ex-offenders at The Fortune Society in New York City. Mrs. Bishop was taught by the look-and-say method and retaught herself to read by phonics-first at the age of thirty-six. This is her story:

I was never a functional illiterate, exactly. I could read well enough to get by, if I bluffed energetically all along the way. But believe me, that's not the life-style anyone would choose, given the choice.

As a pre-schooler, I was bright, gay and outgoing, full of life and full of questions. I was a faculty child, my father a university dean, and our home was full of books and the love of books. My parents read to me regularly, and I listened eagerly. The last thing anybody anticipated was reading difficulty.

But after a few months of public school, things had changed. I had become sober and timid. My eyes hurt all the time. And my progress in reading was very slow. My mother was upset by this development. But my father persuaded her to give the school more time. You see, they had a new system of teaching reading in the school, and he felt sure I would be all right by the end of the year. Any difficulty I was having could be explained by my poor eyesight, which had made it necessary for me to begin wearing glasses at the age of three and a half.

Things went the same during my second and third years in school. Then, on returning from my last day in third grade, I asked my mother, "What is the skin of your teeth?" The teacher had told me that I had passed by that margin. So ended my mother's patience with the public schools. I was transferred to a local Protestant school. They had me repeat third grade, partly to give me a fair chance with French, which began in third grade there, and continued through the upper grades.

I did moderately well at the new school, especially in French, and my reading and writing in English seemed to improve, though they were still "weak." In seventh grade, we started Latin, and again I did very well with it. Again, my reading in English seemed to improve a little. But my spelling was still quite poor, and I was a "reluctant" reader. Despite the eye doctor's best efforts, my eyes still bothered me, and I never read any more than absolutely necessary.

. . . I don't have any memory of personal worry over my reading disability while I was a child. But when I entered the middle teens, I began to find it a burden. A young person who reads well reads widely in fiction and non-fiction, picking up a varied assortment of general information, which supplements the material presented at school. I was completely lacking in this fund of casual information. I began to be embarrassed by the way my ignorance contrasted with my friends' knowledge of the world. Moreover, my parents, who had never made me feel bad about my deficiencies in earlier years, could not conceal their shock and disappointment when they encountered examples of my lack of general knowledge. Even my father began to doubt my potential, in spite of my good school record. But my Latin teacher had been for many years my mother's best friend. She insisted that my intelligence was unusually high, and persuaded my parents to send me to a good college.

Accordingly, I went to Barnard, where I majored in French, and took courses in Spanish, German, and Russian, as well. Again, I used my old tricks to get by. The lecture system was still in force, and I handled all courses given in English by listening to the lecturer and doing a minimum of reading. The foreign language courses were so little problem that I made an average of 3.5 there, whereas my average in courses given in English was only 2.8. (A straight A average works out to 4.0.)

On campus, I was, as usual, constantly embarrassed by my general ignorance. I kept feeling that if only I had the gumption to try harder, I could read as widely and know as much as my peers. But my eyes would not permit that. It never occurred to me then to wonder why I could spend a whole evening devouring a French novel without eye-strain. That fact never penetrated until much later. . . .

. . . I never faced the fact of my reading deficiency until my son Peter was almost through second grade. My husband and I were beginning to be concerned over Peter's reading by then. He still wanted us to read his comic books to him after almost two years of "satisfactory progress" in school. At the spring parent conferences, his teacher told me she was trying one of the books recommended by Rudolf Flesch in his famous book, *Why Johnny Can't Read.* I had heard much about this book, but, true to my deficiency, had never "had time" to read it. Since it appeared to be having a direct impact on Peter, however, I heaved a sigh and buckled down to find out what Flesch was up to.

. . . For me, all this was a weird mixture of news and old story. I knew all about phonics and how to sound out in French, Latin, Spanish, German, and Russian. That's why reading in those languages came so easy. But it was news of the most startling and illuminating sort that phonics could work in English. A detailed reading of the word lists at the back of the book convinced me that English phonics was only slightly more complicated than French, and French is no problem at all, when you know the French letter-sounds.

I was fascinated by English phonics, and began to play with it in every spare moment. I didn't have too many of those, since my daughter Molly was four at the time. But I made every one of them count. My game was to take any handy bit of print and sound out every word strictly by the spelling, noticing all the regular spellings and all the irregular ones, and seeing where context was really needed to help identify a word.

I enjoyed this game for about three weeks. Then suddenly, I couldn't play it properly any more. The meaning of what I was sounding out kept coming through so strongly that it distracted my attention from the game. Well, no toy remains shiny forever. I decided to stop fooling around and start catching up on my neglected reading.

I was in the habit of grabbing one solid half-hour for myself during Molly's morning at nursery school. On this occasion I got a cup of coffee and a stack of reading material, more than enough to last me; set the kitchen timer, and sat down at my ease. That morning, I finished my whole supply of reading matter, and the timer had not rung. I thought it was broken. But my watch said only 15 minutes had passed. Was my watch broken, too? I found the timer still purring away, and agreeing with my industriously ticking watch. It was my own internal time-sense that was out of kilter. In 15 minutes, I had read what would normally have taken me more than twice that time. What's more, I was sure of what all of it had said, an entirely novel experience. I had finally learned, at the age of 36, to read my native language!

Ever since then, I have read well and rapidly, and with the comprehension and recall that were so lacking before. I now read ten times as much as I used to, and enjoy every minute of it. Better still, my eyes never hurt any more, because now I know how to use them for reading. Best of all, I no longer feel guilty and baffled by my general ignorance. Much of it has been overcome, and I know that what remains is not my fault, but the fault of those who introduced the word method, that "new reading system," into the school I attended for the first three grades.

7

"We Do Teach Phonics"

The look-and-say educators say, "We do teach phonics." This is a false claim. They don't teach phonics the way the word is commonly used; they teach only a small part of it; and they teach it the wrong way.

First of all, let's look at the meaning of the word *phonics*. Webster's *New Collegiate Dictionary* (1973) says, "A method of teaching beginners to read and pronounce words by learning the phonetic value of letters, letter groups and esp. syllables."

The key phrase here is "a method." That means phonics is a method or system of teaching reading—*not* one of several aids or approaches or strategies, but *a method*. The child learns phonics and by doing so learns how to read.

For the look-and-say educators this statement is a red flag. They can't stand it. It drives them mad. No, no, they say over and over again, phonics is *not* a complete system. It's just one of several approaches, and the last and poorest one at that. Professor A. Sterl Artley, co-author of the Scott, Foresman look-and-say readers, puts it like this: "Phonic cues are only aids to word identification and not a method to teach reading." (This is from a disdainful article, "Phonics Revisited," which appeared in the February 1977 issue of *Language Arts*.)

So right at the start you have an enormous gulf. The phonics-firsters say phonics is *the* way to teach reading, while the look-and-say people say it's just one of several aids to word recognition.

Now let's have a look at *how much* phonics the look-and-say readers give to children. In contrast to the phonics-first texts, which teach *all* of phonics, look-and-say materials teach only a small part. As I said earlier, Houghton Mifflin, for instance, teaches about 12 percent of all the phonic items before it starts children on reading. Most other look-and-say systems teach even less.

And what do they offer *after* the reading starts? The answer to that is, As little as possible. Not 100 percent, not 90 percent, not 80 percent, but maybe 25 percent or 20 percent. Since they despise the whole business and offer it only to pacify the public, they're determined to keep it to a minimum. The child, they say, doesn't need phonics. It's bad for him. It slows down reading. It's inefficient. It's distracting. It's a complete nuisance. Let's shield the child from the nasty stuff as much as we can.

You don't believe me? Let me prove it to you.

Here's Professor Martha Dallmann, senior author of the reading instruction text *The Teaching of Reading* (fifth edition, 1978):

> Often the method by which an individual has been taught to recognize words plays an important role in reading rate. The person who habitually analyzes words by phonic methods will have slower habits of word recognition than one who has learned to analyze words only if he cannot quickly identify them as wholes. This fact . . . suggests that misuse of phonics is detrimental to speed of reading. Phonics is an important aid to word recognition only when faster methods fail to bring results.

Or take Professor Arthur Heilman, author of the reading instruction text *Principles and Practices of Teaching Reading*:

> Learning to read is a very complicated task. From the very beginning, the learner attempting to identify unfamiliar words should look for and accept help from all available clues. This simultaneous usage of all options helps simplify beginning reading. While it is occasionally true that phonics will be the one key that works, this is not true all of the time. Applying letter-sound analysis should be held to a minimum.

Professor Artley, in the article I quoted before, sums it up in a neat phrase: " 'Sounding out' the word is cumbersome, time consuming, and unnecessary. Like the appendix, its usefulness is a vestige of the past."

So the cry is heard throughout the land, "Teach only a minimum of phonics!" How little? For the answer to that question the educators needed research, data, statistical tables. So they studied the matter in detail and started a little subscience to make sure teachers won't overburden children's minds by giving them too much phonics.

There's now a complete line of research on how to minimize phonics.

The story begins with a now famous article by Professor Theodore Clymer, senior author of the Ginn & Company look-and-say readers, in the January 1963 *Reading Teacher*.

The article was called "The Utility of Phonic Generalizations in the Primary Grades." (*Generalizations* is Professor Clymer's fancy word for rules.) Those rules, he found, don't always apply. So why teach all of them to beginning readers? Let's drop all those that aren't absolutely necessary.

Professor Clymer drew up a list of 121 phonic "generalizations." Where did he get that list? He went through four widely sold look-and-say series and collected the rules they contained. Some of them offered just a few, some a little more. Not one of them even approached Clymer's combined list of 121—not to speak of the total phonic inventory of 181 items I mentioned earlier.

From those 121 phonic rules, Professor Clymer selected 45. Why 45? "The selection was somewhat arbitrary," he wrote.

Next he drew up a list of some 2,600 words drawn from the four look-and-say series through third grade plus the Gates Reading Vocabulary for the Primary Grades. This means that the words chosen to test the usefulness of the phonic rules were only those spoonfed to small children by the look-and-say educators.

Next, Professor Clymer figured the "percent of utility" of his 45 phonic rules for the 2,600 words on his list. For that, he had to decide what was a "reasonable degree of application." Again he used an arbitrary figure. He fixed that cutoff point at 75 percent.

There's a table in Professor Clymer's article that shows the utility of those phonic rules. Only 18 of his 45 rules turned out to be useful by his 75 percent standard. The rest of them fell under the ax. Among them were the ones about silent *e* (only 63 percent useful), long *e* at the end of a word as in *he* or *be* (74 percent useful) and *igh* as in *high* (only 71 percent useful).

While he was at it, Professor Clymer also threw out all those phonic rules that applied to less than 20 words in the first- to third-grade readers. This again yielded a nice harvest of "unnecessary" rules—silent *k* as in *knife*, silent *w* as in *write*, *-ture* as in *picture*, *-tion* as in *station*, and some others. Out with them.

After Professor Clymer's great breakthrough, there was no stopping the educational researchers. His discovery was followed up by Professors Fry (1964), Bailey (1965), Emans (1966), Burmeister (1966), and a summary article again by Burmeister (1968). By the time of Professor Burmeister's summary article on "Usefulness of Phonic Generalizations," the count of useful phonic rules was down to thirteen. She included only those rules that "seemed most useful."

The look-and-say publishers were, of course, happy to accept the fruits of this research. By now I estimate that on the average they offer 20 to 25 percent of the phonic inventory—the 26 letters plus the 13 to 18 rules sifted out by Clymer, Emans, Bailey, Fry, and Burmeister.

And how do they teach their mini-phonics? Here we're at last at the nub of the whole problem. They *don't* teach it. They mention the phonic items and then go right on teaching words by look-and-say.

Let me explain. If you use phonics as *the* method of teaching reading, you teach children the alphabetic code. You do this step by step, in easy stages. At each step, you teach sounding out and blending. Then, at each step, you give the children plenty of material to practice on. When you teach them the short *o*, you give them a hundred words or more with short *o* to read aloud again and again until the pronunciation of short *o* has become fully automatic. You do the same thing with short *u* and *ch* and *th* and *ight* and *ou* and *mps*—through the whole inventory of 181 items until it's all firmly fixed in the pupil's subconscious mind. Sounding out and blending practicing—there's no other way. It's like practicing scales on the piano or practicing driving until you're good enough for the road test.

But the look-and-say books don't do this. They tell the teacher to present a phonic item to the children—*and then teach it by look-and-say.*

Here, for example, is a little segment on teaching phonics from the Harcourt Brace Jovanovich teacher's guide for the reader *World of Surprises* (1979):

> *Phonics:* Write the words *Ben, big,* and *hop* and have pupils identify the vowel in each word. Say the following pairs of words. Have pupils name the letter that stands for the vowel sound in both words.
>
> | | |
> |---|---|
> | *bed, hen* | *hit, fin* |
> | *sock, mop* | *get, went* |
> | *kid, sip* | *lot, stop* |
>
> For a challenging activity, distribute copies of the exercise on page 250 of this Teachers Edition. Then give the following directions: *"Read the words in each column* and underline the letters that stand for the same sound in each word. Then write the word that makes sense in each sentence."

I looked up page 250. It contained a list of 12 words like *wet, Betsy, knock* and *socks,* plus six fill-in sentences such as "That girl's name is _____." The name *Betsy* was the only listed word with a capital initial, so there was no doubt it was the word that completed the sentence "That girl's name is _____."

This is the way Harcourt Brace Jovanovich teaches children to "decode" the short vowels *e, i,* and *o.*

Or let's look at how Scott, Foresman look-and-say readers handle phonics. Page 56 of *Calico Caper* (1978 edition) is a "skills" page that deals with vowels. Its title is "Hope Helps." Then follow these two sentences: "The letters *a* and *o* are *vowel* letters. A vowel letter stands for more than one sound." Next is the beginning of the so-called story: "It was dark on the farm. Hope had to wake up. She washed her face. She drank milk and ate. She went to the barn."

After that, the text says: "You saw these words: *dark, had, wake, farm, drank, face.*"

Next follow four more sentences of the "story" and "You saw these words: *corn, got, Hope, for, lots, bone.*"

On the following page the children are told: "Words like *dark* and *corn* usually have an *r-controlled* vowel sound. Words like *had* and *got* usually have a *short* vowel sound. Words like *wake* and *bone* usually have a *long* vowel sound."

Further down on the page are four brief sentences entitled "Practice skills" that contain the words *porch, not, Jane, yard,* and *grass*.

In the accompanying teacher's manual the teacher is told how to handle that page: "Read the first sentence as pupils follow in their books. Explain that a vowel letter followed by *r* usually stands for an *r*-controlled vowel sound. Say, "Which vowel letter is followed by *r* in *dark?* Which vowel letter is followed by *r* in *corn?*"

This gives you an idea of how Scott, Foresman teaches phonics. Mind you, it's the first introduction of the *ar* and *or* sounds to the children. They are given four words—*dark, farm, corn* and *for*—mixed in with eight others they're supposed to memorize at the same time. Then they're given "practice skills," the words *porch* and *yard*, mixed in with four other words to learn—*not, Jane, grass,* and *rose.*

I don't want to be unfair. There's also something "for pupils who need more guided practice or reteaching in using vowels." For those the teacher is instructed to "write *car, fork; cat, fox; cake, froze* on the board. Have the children read the words aloud and name the vowel sound in each word. Encourage children to dictate sentences using the words on the board. Write these sentences on the board."

To call this kind of teaching inadequate is a gross understatement. Remember, it's the first time the children learn about *ar* and *or*. They're given three *ar* words and three *or* words. "Those who need more guided practice" get one more *ar* word and one more *or* word. These words are mixed in with 16 other words to be memorized and some 50 words making up the so-called story. (In a phonics-first text the children would get about a hundred *ar* words and a hundred *or* words to practice on until the pronunciations of *ar* and *or* are firmly fixed in their subconscious minds.)

Now let's have a look at Ginn & Company. Page 134 of the teacher's manual for *A Duck Is a Duck* (1978) is headed "Decoding." It says:

> Structural analysis: The pupils will decode words with graphemic bases *in* and *ine*. Write the following sentences on the chalkboard: "It is a fine line. We can win a tin pin." Review the graphemic bases *in* and *ine* by having pupils read the sentences orally.
>
> Write the following on the chalkboard:
> *I can see (nine) (pin) ducks at the park.*
> *That red bike is (win) (mine).*

There follow two more sentences to write on the board. Then the manual continues: "Ask volunteers to read each sentence and the answer choices. Have other volunteers circle the word that finishes each sentence. Then have the children point out the graphemic bases *in* and *ine* and compare the bases."

Further down on the page the manual says, "For practice in decoding words with the graphemic bases *in* and *ine*, distribute activity page 45."

I looked up activity page 45. It showed five pictures with five sentences that offered choices of *in* and *ine* words. Number 5 had a picture of a little girl looking at a cake with nine candles. The sentence said, "Kim is (din) (nine)."

I assure you I have not maliciously distorted the Ginn method of teaching phonics. This is it. They give the children *in* and *ine*—a small fraction of the important phonic rule that deals with silent *e* and long vowels—and then wrap up a few *in* and *ine* words in some contexts. Instead of teaching or even simply telling the children anything about the principle involved, they ask them whether it makes more sense to say, "That red bike is win" or "That red bike is mine."

Finally, there's little Kim, who is not "din" but "nine." The number of candles on her birthday cake proves it. How does all this help children to learn about silent *e*? Ask the people at Ginn & Company.

I've gone through volume after volume of the look-and-say teacher's manuals and found that their teaching of phonics—or "decoding"—is always the same. They pick an item from the phonic inventory, list one, two, four, six sample words, and *then teach those words by putting them in a context*. This is exactly the same as what they do with all other words they teach children to memorize.

It may be good enough to help them recognize 1,500 words in four years, but it doesn't do the job real phonics teaching is supposed to do—teach them the alphabetic code so they can read fluently for the rest of their lives.

But of course the look-and-say people don't admit that phonics is necessary. All anyone needs, they say, is "an effective decoding strategy." This is the heading of a full page that's printed in the front of all primary Houghton Mifflin teacher's manuals. Here is what it says, in part:

> At the prereading level, students learn to use context together with letter-sound associations for consonants in the initial position to decode an unfamiliar printed word form into a spoken word that is familiar in sound and meaning. *With this decoding strategy, students do not need to rely on a procedure of sounding each letter to read an unknown word.* The use of context limits the possibilities to a word that makes sense. Using context together with some letter-sound associations will enable students to decode words for themselves. . . .
>
> . . . Students are ready to begin reading stories . . . when they have mastered the decoding strategy involving the use of context together with the letter-sound associations for 22 consonant sounds. . . .
>
> . . . As they progress . . . they learn an increasing number of phonic elements and thereby increase their efficiency in decoding words. . . . By the end of [third grade] students have learned . . . a decoding strategy that will enable them to read words that are unfamiliar only in their printed form.

The phrase "decoding strategy" is now universally used by the look-and-say educators. All the teacher's manuals and reading instruction texts are full of it. Phonics is out, decoding strategy is in.

Let's look at it. What does *strategy* mean? It means a plan or policy you use to win a battle or a game. It implies that the success of the child's strategy is uncertain—he may either win or lose. He may be forever struggling to read accurately what's on the page.

And *decoding?* By now the look-and-say people have used the word so often that it has almost lost its original meaning. Decoding means translating into intelligible language something that's written in code. When you're faced with something written in code, you must first break the code—as the Allies did in World War II with the German and Japanese codes. Once you've broken the code, you can decode all further messages by simply having the codebook at your elbow and looking up every word.

In look-and-say jargon *decoding* is now used as if it meant code-breaking. The poor child, whenever an unfamiliar—or forgotten—word appears on a page, has to do the code-breaking job all over again, working slowly and laboriously from the first few letters and the context. He may or may not succeed. He may make a mistake, he may give up on or skip difficult words, or he may rush on, vaguely conscious that what he has read isn't quite what's on the page.

This is how over half the American population reads now, thanks to the fact that educators are determined not to teach them the code.

They have devised thousands of ingenious exercises to train children in this insane method of reading. They make them complete such sentences as "There are fish in the l_____," "The package was tied up with str_____," or "I went to the zoo and saw a kangaroo j_____." The child is praised if he obligingly reads, "There are fish in the lake," "The package was tied up with string," and "I went to the zoo and saw a kangaroo jump."

Unfortunately—or fortunately—life is not as simple and dull as all that. Real-life sentences are apt to read "There are fish in the lagoon," "The package was tied up with straps," and "I went to the zoo and saw a kangaroo just as tall as you are."

A child taught by look-and-say will go through life and miss all the interesting and unexpected stuff in print. He's been trained to assume that what comes next is always the expected word and therefore never discovers the fact that, as often as not, printed matter takes surprising turns.

In 1979, when Pope John Paul II visited the United States, *New York Times* columnist Tom Wicker wrote, "The most impassioned theme of his visit was that 'in the light of the parable of Christ, riches and freedom create a special responsibility. . . .' "

A look-and-say-taught reader, trained to guess words from the first few letters and the context, surely would have misread the word *impassioned* as *important.* Look-and-say educators will naturally say, So what? But I say passionately that accuracy is important. To sacrifice it needlessly is a sin.

But even that is not all. Children are not only trained in inaccuracy, they're trained not to look at the words on the page if they can help it. There's a book called *Strategies for Identifying Words* by Professor Dolores Durkin that tells teachers to train children to think of other words *first* before they look at what's on the page. On page 83 Professor Durkin imagines the thought process of a "successful decoder" when faced with the sentence *They make belts out of plastic:*

> Well, it isn't "leather" because that begins with *l.* My mother has a straw belt, but it isn't "straw" either. It looks like a root. I'll divide it between *s* and *t.* There couldn't be more than two syllables because there are only two vowels. Let's see—*p, l, a, s.* One vowel and it's not at the end of the syllable. I'll try the short sound for *a.* That would be: *ă, plă, plăs.* Plăs? I can't think of any word that starts that way. I'd better see what the second syllable sounds like. One vowel again, and it's not at the end. That would probably be a short sound for *i,* and *c* isn't followed by any letter, so I'll try the hard sound for that. That would be: *i, ti, tik. Plas-tik.* Oh, sure, Plastic! I'm surprised I didn't think of that right away because so many things are made of plastic.

Professor Durkin makes the following comment:

> Just described is a child who was not about to carry on a letter-by-letter analysis of *plastic* if it wasn't necessary, which is exactly right. (In some classrooms, phonics is so overemphasized that children can be found analyzing words they are already able to read!) Because nothing

about the spelling of *plastic* lent support to either
"leather" or "straw," this child temporarily abandoned
the sense of context to turn to visual cues.

I can assure you that this passage from Professor Durkin's
book is not an isolated, extreme aberration. It's typical of what
you'll find in thousands of look-and-say readers, manuals, and
texts.

Until quite recently nobody bothered to challenge the theory
behind all that "decoding strategy" nonsense. Is it really true
that you can normally guess the next word from the context
and the initial letter or two? In a 1980 paper Dr. Philip Gough
of the University of Texas and two of his graduate students
conducted a little experiment. They asked a faculty colleague
"to guess—one at a time—the first one hundred words of each
of ten ordinary reading selections. After each guess, we read
the correct word, and then repeated, at our subject's request,
the entire text up to and including that word. Thus he had
available, at every point, the entire preceding context to assist
him."

The report continues: "Our intelligent, well-educated
reader, given unlimited time to select a word, can predict only
about one word in four. . . . We would submit that this must
be near the upper boundary of predictability, and the accuracy
which would be achieved in real time by the reader must be
far, far less."

So, since three out of four predictions are normally wrong
"it is clear that the net effect of prediction . . . cannot be to
facilitate word recognition: the cumulative effect of the more
frequent false predictions would be to swamp the advantage
of the occasional correct one."

It seems to me that Dr. Gough's findings confirm the com-
mon-sense view: if you tell a child he should always think about
leather and straw before reading the word *plastic* off the page,
you'll ruin his chances of ever becoming a fluent reader.

A few weeks after I'd finished writing this chapter, the following irresistible excerpt from Thomas H. Middleton's column
in the *Saturday Review* came my way:

I encountered a product of the word method of instruction a few months ago. I had taken some quite spectacular

shots of the autumn foliage in New Hampshire last fall, and a few of the four-by-six prints were so good that I had them blown up to eleven-by-fourteens. One of the enlargements came back as a badly faded version of the smaller print, so I took it back to the camera shop. The young man who waited on me was a recent high school graduate whom I knew slightly and who seemed bright and articulate. I showed him the two prints and he agreed the large one was very short on color. He said he'd have the lab do it over, and he added, "We'll put in the four-by-six as a guide print." He did so, then he wrote on the envelope: To light. Guild print inclosed.

"To" for "too" is bad, but more or less understandable. "Inclosed" is an unusual but acceptable variant of "Enclosed." But "guild" for "guide"? I could understand "guyed" or "gyde" or even "gide," but to put an unsounded *L* in there is so thoroughly puzzling as to indicate some sort of brain dysfunction—perhaps the very brain dysfunction implied in the term *dyslexia*. Oh, well. At least he got the first three letters right.

8

"No One Method Is Best"

Perhaps the most fashionable of the educators' alibis is the one that says phonics may be best for some children, but look-and-say is best for others. Dr. Howe, the U.S. ex-Commissioner of Education, as usual furnished the most pompous formulation: "Children learn in different ways, and it is important to find how a particular child can be helped to learn, rather than assuming there is one method for all."

This sounds very grand in its Olympian evenhandedness. Teach the more auditory children by phonics, but don't deprive the more visual ones of their right to be taught by look-and-say.

Laymen who read or hear this argument get the impression that our wise educators carefully test children to see whether they'll learn better by phonics or look-and-say and then teach them in the way that best suits each child.

Of course anyone who has ever seen an ordinary American classroom knows this isn't so. Reading instruction goes on day after day; the children sit in their circles, taking turns in reading aloud the "stories" in their Houghton Mifflin, Ginn, or Scott, Foresman readers. Instruction in true phonics, as I showed in the last chapter, isn't anywhere in sight.

So how come this is such a popular alibi? Where's the catch? I was much puzzled by this and did quite some detective work to find out. I found the answer in Professor Joseph Wepman's article in the March 1960 *Elementary School Journal*. It is called "Auditory Discrimination, Speech and Reading."

Professor Wepman, co-author of the Scott, Foresman look-and-say readers, starts with the difference between *wreath* and *reef*. Small children, he says, often have difficulty in distinguishing such words because they can't tell the sounds of *th* and *f* apart. Among children under eight, he writes, "their number is felt to be great." So, because they're hampered in learning to read through the auditory "pathway," let's teach them by look-and-say and forget about phonics.

Now, since reading is taught in the first three grades, this pushes phonics out of regular classrooms and makes it a special tool for "auditory" children whose visual perception isn't good enough for look-and-say. Since there are only a handful of those around, this practically eliminates phonics from general use.

Professor Wepman constructed a time-consuming and expensive test to check children's auditory perception and Alibi No. 3 was on its way.

By 1964 Professor Wepman, in a second article, was hitting full stride and described his idea in rather grandiose terms:

> The teaching of reading should be child-centered rather than method-centered. The question should not be whether visual sight reading or phonics or any other method is the approach to use, but which children among all those to be taught should be taught by which method. No method should be considered incorrect for any member of a group because it has not reached all of the children. . . . Before we explore whether a given child or group of children should be taught by sight-recognition methods or by phonic methods, we should determine which of the perceptual building blocks he can utilize best in the integrative conceptualizing process of gaining meaning from the printed page.

Soaring even higher into the stratosphere of educational jargon, Professor Wepman concluded:

> The modality approach to reading—by differentiating the perceptual levels of transmitting input signals and their ability, in the intermodal transfer, to arouse the associations necessary for integration and thus meaning—only nominates the directions of individualized training. It permits each child to function in the manner for which he is best equipped. It predicates the need for understanding each child as a total organism complete within himself.

All of which means, in plain English, "Lots of children under eight have trouble hearing the difference between such words as *wreath* and *reef.* Let's make sure these children are taught by look-and-say rather than phonics."

Soon Professor Wepman's theory became widely accepted. In 1966 a book appeared with the revealing title *Predicting Reading Failure* by De Hirsch, Jansky, and Langford. De Hirsch and her co-authors gave a group of fifty-three New York City kindergartners a battery of tests, among them Wepman's Test of Auditory Discrimination. They found only three among the fifty-three who were poor on the auditory perception but good visualizers. As it happened, these three were taught by look-and-say in first grade and did all right. There were also seven children who were good on the auditory side and poor on the visual side. Five of them happened to be taught phonics and did fine in first grade. The other two unfortunately were taught by look-and-say and flunked.

This was hardly scientific proof for Wepman's theory of "modality matching," but De Hirsch and her co-authors recommended the practice anyway.

The time was ripe for a serious, properly controlled experiment to find out once and for all whether there was anything to all this. The person who undertook the job was Dr. Barbara Bateman, then at the University of Illinois. (She is now at the University of Oregon.)

Dr. Bateman made arrangements with the school system of Highland Park, an affluent Chicago suburb. Children in eight kindergarten classes were given a battery of tests. They were assigned to four first-grade classes that served as controls, and four others. There they were distributed as follows: Children with good auditory and poor visual discrimination were put in one class, where they were taught by look-and-say (Scott, Foresman) and in another where they were taught by phonics (Lippincott). The same was done with children who'd tested high on visual perception and low on auditory perception.

After they'd completed first grade, the 95 children in the experiment were given reading achievement tests plus a spelling test, consisting of 12 regular words and 6 nonsense words.

The results of Dr. Bateman's experiment were quite a surprise to her. The "modality matching" idea didn't work out at all. There was absolutely no statistical proof that "auditory" children learned better by phonics or that "visual" children learned better by look-and-say. Professor Wepman's ingenious theory had fallen flat on its face.

But this wasn't all. Dr. Bateman inadvertently had added one more to the over one hundred studies that showed that phonics was superior to look-and-say. *All* the children in the Highland Park schools who'd learned with the Lippincott phonics system did better than the children who'd been taught by the Scott, Foresman brand of look-and-say. On the average, at the end of first grade, they were 3⅓ months ahead. In spelling, the difference was even more striking. The phonics-trained children on the average got 6.8 of the 18 test words right; the look-and-say-trained children could correctly spell only an average of 2.8.

Dr. Bateman also divided the children into "good" readers—those who scored at or above a 3.9 reading grade level—and "poor" readers—those who scored below 2.9. (Yes, even the slowest first-graders in those affluent Highland Park schools read at the end-of-second-grade level after they'd finished first grade.)

The result was again astonishing. Among the 48 children who'd been taught by phonics there were only 2 poor readers; among the 47 look-and-say students—same age, same high IQ—there were 16. There were 14 *good* readers among the phonics-trained group and only 2 among those exposed to look-and-say.

The whole experiment added up to a crushing defeat for Professor Wepman's theory and another triumph for phonics in its long battle against look-and-say.

Understandably, the look-and-say people and the people at Scott, Foresman in particular were not too happy with Dr. Bateman's findings. Surely, they said, something should be done to wipe this annoying research finding off the map.

So they called on one of their big guns, their senior author and professor emerita at the University of Chicago, Professor Helen M. Robinson. Professor Robinson was to do a great unassailable piece of research that would sink Dr. Bateman without a trace.

Scott, Foresman dug deep into their Gray Research Fund,

named of course after Dr. William S. Gray, the revered father
of Dick and Jane, and hired four research assistants, plus several
others who stood by to help out at peak testing periods.

Armed with this ample supply of money and her sizable
crew, Professor Robinson went into the schools of Lake Bluff,
Arlington Heights, Wilmington, and Joliet. Instead of Dr. Bateman's measly bunch of 95 children in Highland Park, Professor
Robinson started out with 448 children in 22 classrooms in
the four Illinois communities. She gave them an even longer
battery of tests than Dr. Bateman at kindergarten age, and
then tested them with "discrepant modalities" at the end of
first grade. Again the children had been split up among regular
look-and-say classes—one taught by Scott, Foresman, the other
by Ginn—and two other classes taught by the classic phonic
text *Reading with Phonics* by Hay-Wingo.

To avoid the influence of the high IQs of the Highland Park
children—average 126—the four communities were chosen because the children came from rural and lower-middle-class
backgrounds. Their average IQ was 105. (The norm is 100.)

At the end of first grade Professor Robinson assembled her
reading scores and drew up her statistical tables. Surprise—
Dr. Bateman had been perfectly right and Professor Wepman's
theory had been disproved again. There was no effect of "modality matching" whatever, and the children in the phonics-
first classes, whatever their auditory or visual capacities, had
outperformed those taught by Ginn and Scott, Foresman.

Professor Robinson couldn't let things go at that point. She
ran the experiment for another year and waited for the results.
But there was a hitch. Many of the teachers "were unaccus-
tomed to giving tests" and their forms had to be thrown away.

Undaunted, Professor Robinson continued the experiment
and waited another year. At the end of the third year, she
and her assistants gave the tests themselves and made sure
they collected them themselves. Then they checked the results
and drew up their tables.

Fate, however, was again unkind to look-and-say. The children, after three years, again refused to confirm Professor Wepman's scheme. Modality matching suffered still another defeat.
As to the overall difference between the effectiveness of phonics-first and look-and-say, phonics-first won again on all counts.

There is no direct statement to that effect in Professor Robinson's thirty-two-page report on her experiment. All she can bring herself to say is, on page 28, "The right half of Table 11 shows the mean scores of the four groups." I looked at that right half of Table 11. Yes indeed, it showed that phonics-first won decisively.

I ought to add that in contrast to Dr. Bateman's experiment, in which the Lippincott series was used as the medium of phonics teaching, Professor Robinson used Hay-Wingo, the simple phonics primer that taught children to read in the first half of the first year—usually before Christmas. So, whatever the phonics-trained children did in the two-and-a-half years after they'd finished their Hay-Wingo primers, their initial thorough training in phonics stuck with them. At the end of third grade they were still able to outperform their Ginn- and Scott, Foresman–trained competitors.

And what did Professor Robinson tell her employers at the end of her unsuccessful mission? Not much. There were two pages of mumbling about further research, proposing that one should try again with larger groups of over 1,000 children, following them up through sixth grade.

One thing more: Professor Robinson also laid to rest Professor Wepman's claim that a "great number" of children under eight suffered from poor auditory perception. Among Robinson's 448 children, there were only 6 percent in that condition.

In his review on reading research (*Reading Teacher*, March 1976) Professor Albert J. Harris, senior author of the Macmillan look-and-say readers, reported sadly that, according to Bateman and Robinson, there was "no relationship between a child's stronger aptitude and success in learning to read by a particular method. "Research," he wrote, "seems to support the use of a multisensory method from which the child can select whatever cues are most helpful to him in learning to identify written or printed words." (Obviously, the method Professor Harris is referring to is "We Do Teach Phonics" look-and-say.) "In regard to remedial teaching," he goes on, "there is insufficient research on this issue to decide the question."

The remedial teaching and special education people needed no encouragement to continue this line of research. After Bateman and Robinson had proved finally that there was absolutely no validity to the whole idea, other researchers went right ahead to try to prove this disproven fact over and over again.

In the fall of 1979 Dr. Judith A. Arter and Dr. Joseph R. Jenkins wrote a definitive review of the whole matter, entitled "Differential Diagnosis—Prescriptive Teaching: A Critical Appraisal." It took them thirty-eight pages in the *Review of Educational Research* to cover the subject. Even so, they had to apologize because the field had grown so enormously that a true survey of all primary sources would have been prohibitive. The new subscience had spread so widely that only a full book could do it real justice. This in spite—or because—of the fact that "research findings seriously challenge the model's validity and suggest that continued advocacy of the model cannot be justified." In other words, vast masses of research had been done even though research had proved conclusively and unanimously that there was absolutely nothing to the whole idea.

Arter and Jenkins had unearthed thirteen more research studies after Bateman and Robinson had done their work. Twelve of those studies again proved conclusively that "modality matching" was a total washout. The thirteenth, by someone named Bursuk in 1979, had been done with tenth graders rather than first graders, and the results with the auditory learners had been carefully rigged by letting them not only read the stories but also listen to them being read aloud.

So Professor Wepman's idea of modality matching had suffered fourteen resounding defeats. Will this be the end? "Not bloody likely," to quote George Bernard Shaw. Look-and-say educators follow the motto "If at first you don't succeed in proving a preconceived idea, repeat the research again and again until everyone gets tired of the whole thing and gives up from sheer exhaustion."

Arter and Jenkins were not only interested in simple research. They also penetrated into the rank and file of the educational profession. They sent a questionnaire to 700 special education elementary school teachers in the state of Illinois. They received 340 completely filled-in questionnaires.

In their letter they had written:

Dear Special Education Teacher:
  We need 7 minutes of your time.
  We are seeking your help in evaluating one aspect of

special education teacher preparation curricula. We are examining the prevalence and utility of the *Modality Model* as employed in teaching. In brief, this model holds that individual children have relative strengths or weaknesses in auditory or visual channels. That is, some children may be described primarily as auditory learners while other children are primarily visual learners. When using this model in teaching, the teacher modifies instructional methods and materials in accord with the child's strengths and weaknesses.

We are sending this questionnaire to a carefully selected, representative group of special education teachers chosen from among all special education teachers in the State of Illinois. Your answers to this questionnaire will help us determine (1) if you use this technique, (2) how useful it has been for you, and (3) the type of children this technique works best or worst with. It is critical that we receive a good return if we are to insure that the results accurately represent current practice.

Please fill out the enclosed questionnaire and return it in the self-addressed, stamped envelope provided. All responses are strictly confidential. If you would like a copy of the results of this survey, please indicate this at the bottom of the questionnaire. Please try to return this questionnaire within two days.

The results of this survey will help us to modify our university's special education curricula, and may influence those of other universities in the State.

Here are some answers from the questionnaire:

Are you familiar with the modality model as we have described it? Yes (87%)

A child's modality strength and weakness should be a main consideration when devising educational prescriptions. Yes (99%)

It is my impression that most of the research on modality shows that we cannot improve children's learning by planning instruction in accord with children's modality strength and weaknesses. Disagree (95%)

Approximately how often do you use the modality model?
                                    Frequently or always (78%)

When I consider modality, I usually try to plan instruction
so that I teach using the strong modality rather than the
weak modality.   Yes (84%)

In my experience, I have gotten better results when I
have modified my instruction in accord with a child's modality assessment.   Yes (94%)

All of which gives you convincing proof that Illinois special
education teachers (a) are wholly unfamiliar with the findings
of research in their profession; (b) blindly continue practices
that have been proven totally wrong; and (c) are convinced
these discredited practices work fine with their children.

Why do they behave like that?

Arter and Jenkins thought about this question. They feel
that teachers "responded to the questionnaire according to
what they thought, through prior training, was educationally
appropriate. . . . Unsupported expert opinion and the teacher
training programs resulting from this opinion, therefore, appear to have a direct and, perhaps, deleterious effect on teacher
behavior."

"Not only are teachers employing an ineffective model," they
add, "but because they have been persuaded that the model
is useful, they are less apt to create variations in instructional
procedures which will result in improved learning."

So ends the sad story of Professor Wepman's modality matching idea. It took fifteen studies—some major, some minor—
to disprove it fully and thoroughly and to show that high-audi-
tory and high-visual children profit equally from the phonics-
first method and should *not* be taught by look-and-say. This
solid bit of scientific fact has been ignored like all the other
solid scientific facts that have proved that look-and-say is a
pernicious, phony method that should have been abandoned
long ago.

Now that we have a whole subindustry of special education
in all its forms, the battle over the modality matching has
shifted to the field of special education. The same stubborn
resistance to scientific proof, the same total unwillingness to

pay any attention whatever to scientific findings persist. They go on modality matching, no matter what utter nonsense it has turned out to be, and they'll be proud that they have employed this latest wrinkle of sophisticated educational technique. Your Johnny doesn't hear the difference between *wreath* and *reef?* Off he goes, the predestined victim of Ginn, Macmillan, Scott, Foresman, etc.

One more word. The good researchers in the reading field— like Drs. Joanna Williams, Michael and Lise Wallach—have known about auditory discrimination for many years. They say, with utter common sense, that children who are no good at this should be trained specially *before* they are taught how to read. By phonics, of course.

9

"English Isn't Phonetic"

In a "fact sheet" sent out by Ginn & Company after the appearance of my *Family Circle* article, one paragraph, which I quoted earlier, says, "Mr. Flesch paints an unrealistic picture of the English language. While the basal reader has words in it which are approximately 80 percent decodable by a phonics process, the real world language is not as regular. Therefore, care must be taken to teach children to decode words in other ways than phonics-first so that they have other strategies to use when phonics fails them."

There are so many things wrong with this paragraph that it will take me a page or two to sort them out.

In the first place, I didn't say 80 percent, I said 87 percent. I used this figure on page 19 of my book *Why Johnny Can't Read*. There I said, the figure "has been established by three or four independent researchers." Among them were Miss Julie Hay and Mr. Charles E. Wingo, who said on page 11 of their teacher's manual for *Reading with Phonics* (Lippincott, now out of print): "Thirteen percent of all English syllables are not phonetic. Eighty-seven percent of all syllables in our language are purely phonetic and the words in which unphonetic syllables occur are in part phonetic. Knowing the phonetic facts about our language, therefore, provides the tool with which pupils may recognize instantly nearly all of our English words."

So the 87 percent—*not* 80 percent—figure applies to *all* English words, not just to the words in the Ginn basal readers, as the Ginn people are trying to insinuate. The English language, according to Hay-Wingo, is 87 percent phonetic, and that's that. That's not only that, but of the remaining 13 percent words, most have just slight differences in their vowel pronunci-

94

ations, but are otherwise perfectly phonetic, such as *gone, friend* and *again.* To say that "in the real world" there are thousands more irregular words that have to be tackled by other "strategies" is—to put it exactly—a blatant lie.

Now then. Much water has flowed under the bridge since Hay and Wingo wrote their primer in 1948. Among other things, there was the invention of the computer.

In 1963, Paul R. Hanna, Jean S. Hanna, Richard E. Hodges, and Edwin H. Rudorf got hold of a government grant for a tremendous computer-assisted project. They picked 17,000 words—15,284 from the Thorndike-Lorge *Teachers' Word Book* of 30,000 words plus an extra 2,026 from the sixth edition of Merriam-Webster's *New Collegiate Dictionary.* They then programmed a computer with all the phonetic spelling rules they could think of and tried to find out how the computer would spell this representative sample of English. The computer performed beautifully, spelling English exactly by all the rules, as long as the programmers didn't make any mistakes. (The programmers, being human, of course did make mistakes, and the computer, following directions, spelled *plaground* instead of *playground.*)

However, the Hannas and their co-workers were interested in spelling rather than reading. With all its glorious successes, the Hanna computer still didn't have the answer to my question, How regular is English for a reader rather than a speller?

For this question Mrs. Margaret Bishop, reading director of the Fortune Society, came to my rescue. Mrs. Bishop is one of God's chosen list-makers. She undertook the job of translating the Hanna computer data into a complete alphabetical list of the 17,000 words, all properly organized with each exception in its proper place. The title of her book is *The ABC's and All Their Tricks.* It throws such a sharp light on our educational Establishment that no commercial publisher took the manuscript and Mrs. Bishop had to publish her book herself.

Anyway, she lent me a precious copy, and I spent a happy afternoon working out the percentage of "decodable" words— that is, words that can be read and pronounced according to known and established phonetic principles. At the end of the afternoon I had my answer. It was 97.4 percent.

Yes, 97.4 percent. English spelling is, according to the

unassailable scientific work of Hanna and Bishop, 97.4 percent phonetic. You are welcome at any time to check the computer data of the Hannas and the painstaking handiwork of Mrs. Bishop—plus the simple computation that I did in a long, fascinating afternoon.

What does it mean, 97.4 percent phonetic? It means that if you take almost any English word, properly spelled or fantastically misspelled, you'll be able to read it if you've learned to read by phonics. If the word is *obsequiousness*, it'll be easy as pie for you, and if it is *okapi* it will also be easy as pie. Even if someone writes to you about an Arab *chic*, you'll know he means a *sheik*. A *Monday Thursday* will reveal itself as a *Maundy Thursday*. And *kee* of course means *quay* or *key*.

As long as you try to read by phonics, you just sail along, undisturbed by any spelling mistakes your fellow citizens may be inclined to make. You know what you know. Just read along what's on the page. Once you've learned the phonetic key to reading your problem is solved.

For the first few weeks or months of learning how to read by phonics, you need a little help by having the words and letters arranged in such an order that you won't get confused, but after that short period is over, you're on your own—gloriously, independently on your own. I love the sentence that appears on page xi of the *Foundation Level B* teacher's manual of the Open Court reading system (at the end of the first half of the first year): "Once *Foundation* is completed, no vocabulary control is required."

Think of this and of the years and years—the junior high school years and senior high school years and college years—when look-and-say keeps on and on controlling the vocabulary. The phonics-trained student is free—he can read *obsequiousness* and *Quetzalcoatl* and *xerophthalmia* off the page.

(If you want to start arguing about meaning at this point, please wait for the next chapter—Alibi No. 5.)

And now, once this point is settled—and I hope it's settled for good—let's talk about so-called sight words. As you may have noticed, so far there has been no mention of sight words at all. A student learns the phonic rules and the words exemplifying them—*cat, bat, mat*, and *fake, drape, shame*—and by the time he gets to the end of the 181-item phonic inventory, he can read English.

Yes, you say, but what about all those sight words? A teacher—a pleasant, unaggressive one—wrote to me, "In kindergarten children are introduced to the letters and their sounds. In first grade I continue to teach by phonics, in which I introduce certain basic sight vocabulary. Some of these words cannot be easily decoded through simple phonics rules (ex. *the, said, come, one, four, who, their*). As the child begins reading he uses both methods in his own way. Some children depend more on phonics, some memorize words more easily. The child then has both methods at his disposal."

It all sounds so reasonable, doesn't it? Here is an obviously nice person trying to do her best to teach children to read. What's wrong with an eminently sane approach?

What's wrong, of course, is that the child will never learn to read this way. Once you have a language that's 97.4 percent phonetically regular, the thing to do is to teach it by telling the child, one after another, about the 181 rules, and then he can read. As soon as you interrupt your teaching to tell the children about some irregular words like *some, one, are,* or *was,* you've started the poor child on the path to confusion and the scheme falls apart.

I began to wonder what I'd done with those so-called sight words when I wrote *Why Johnny Can't Read,* which by all accounts works like a charm. Well, after some searching, I found page 100. There I'd written, "You don't have to wait a whole year, though, before you can give your child stories to read. Let him learn how it feels to read; if you teach him phonics right along, he won't be confused by 'unphonetic,' words like *was* and *done.*"

And that's all there is to it. At some point, when you feel the time has come, start your child on reading stories—real stories, I mean, not the look-and-say pap—and he won't hesitate a minute to pronounce *was* as *wuz* and *done* as *dun.*

I looked up some other simple systems that teach children to read in a few weeks or months and found the same simple treatment of sight words. In *Johnny Still Can't Read—But You Can Teach Him at Home* by Kathryn Diehl and G. K. Hodenfield, page 29 says, *"Sight Words:* In teaching your child to read, you should have a list of the relatively few but constantly needed words which don't follow phonetic pronunciation rules. Here is such a list: *are, come, could, do, does, eight, once, one, put, said, some, their, there, they, two, were, where, who, work, would, you, your."*

In *Professor Phonics Gives Sound Advice* by Monica Foltzer, page 11, I found, "A suggested list of [common sight words] is *was, were, is, to, of, for, the, a, I, you."*

In *The Writing Road to Reading* by Romalda Bishop Spalding and Walter T. Spalding I found no special list of sight words at all, but an occasional remark, as at *says:* "We say *sez,"* and at *heart:* "We say *hart."*

The point is that the whole issue of sight words comes up only because the look-and-say people insist they must immediately have the children read stories. Dumb stories, inane stories, but stories there must be, otherwise the child is "bored" and lacks "motivation." The phonics people go ahead and teach children to read, relying on the sheer thrill of learning the alphabetic code—one of the great wonders of the world—to fascinate the children until they can hardly wait to be told that *u* makes *yoo.*

But the look-and-say people don't know about children. They think they must let them read stories with lots of *was's* and *said's* that will make them jump up and down with joy and excitement.

I spent an hour or so assembling the most common sight words that play such an enormous role in the look-and-say method of teaching. I immediately found ten words the lazy American tongue likes to muffle—*a, come, does, done, none, of, some, the, was,* and *were.* Next were another ten with an unusually pronounced vowel: *again, against, been, friend, gone, have, money, ready, said,* and *says.*

There are 21 more words of a similar type—*any, buy, could, do, eye, many, once, one, put, sew, shoe, should, their, there, to, two, where, who, whose, women,* and *would.*

Finally add nine more words—*answer, breakfast, beautiful, buy, laugh, only, people, pretty,* and *Wednesday.*

And that's the whole list—except, of course, for the famous spelling-bee words of which we are so proud—*acoustics, asthma, awry, boatswain, choir, colonel, fuchsia, indict, khaki, plaid, sergeant, solder, sieve, thyme,* and *victuals.*

And for that ridiculously short list we should teach our children to read English like Chinese, in spite of the fact it is 97.4 percent decodable?

Many years ago, when my older children were quite small, I owned a lovely big St. Bernard dog. I named him Rigi, after the famous Swiss mountain. I seem to remember that I once traced his name in the sand—RIGI—and explained to the children that this spelled his name—*reeguee.*

I was reminded of this by an interview with Professor Kenneth Goodman, the senior author of the Scott, Foresman basal look-and-say readers, that appeared on March 30, 1980 in the *Arizona Republic.* "One of the strategies that we teach kids," he told the reporter, "is the blank strategy. Say 'blank' and go ahead. What happens is that if a word is important to the story, about the third or fourth time the kids have got it, because each successive context gives them more clues."

Professor Goodman, of course, has gained national fame with his "miscue analysis" and "hypothesis-testing strategy of reading." What would he have done about Rigi, I wonder? Let the reader call him "blank" the first time, "Rex" the second, "Rover" the third, "Fido" the fourth time, and perhaps "Kenneth" the fifth? Hypothesis testing, my eye. Testing against what criterion? Surely not the alphabetic code, which is now kept secret from most of the American population. The customs of the country, perhaps? Fashions in dog naming around the mid-1940s? Degrees of whimsy? Knowledge of Swiss geography?

Don't laugh. There are educational libraries full of books and articles about miscue theory, hypothesis testing, error-correcting frequencies, and variations of technique—a whole panoply of elaborate modern science, not unlike nuclear physics in its outer reaches. I have an article in my files that tells about a six-week course in miscue evaluation, filled with statistics on the students' successes in improving children's "miscue strategies."

The sum total of these misdirected energies boggles the mind.

10

"Word Calling Isn't Reading"

In the early 1940s Dr. Robert H. Seashore of Northwestern University made one of the most sensational discoveries in the history of psychology. He found that the average six-year-old enters school with a speaking and listening vocabulary of over 24,000 words.

Dr. Seashore knew very well that he'd thrown a live bomb into the educational establishment.

> The results of the test were startling [he wrote]. Most of the common beliefs about vocabulary are grossly in error. . . . Note for example that the average growth in total vocabulary was 5,000 words per year from the first through the twelfth grades. . . . What does this do to some of the series of school readers . . . which are based on the assumption that children can master, on the average, only about 500 new words per year?
>
> As a matter of fact, the situation is still worse. . . . The results indicate that it is possible to double the rate of vocabulary growing simply by interesting children in learning the significant things about new words. . . . One might almost say that children's vocabularies have been developed in spite of, rather than through the aid of, certain common methods of instruction and those textbooks which limit vocabulary to the extreme.

Having thrown his bomb and pointed out its enormous significance, Seashore briefly surveyed the history of vocabulary estimates:

> The first source of misinformation is an early study by an English lay writer, Dean Farrar, who simply lay on his

back in his yard one afternoon and listened to the conversation of a group of fruit pickers in the yard next door.
At the end of that time he made a guess that the vocabularies of these rural men did not exceed 100 words each.

The second source of misinformation is based upon
counts . . . of the total number of different words used
by writers in all of their published works—Milton 11,000,
Shakespeare 15,000, Victor Hugo 20,000. This involves
a whole series of fallacious assumptions. . . .

The third main source of misinformation is the finding
of L. M. Terman that . . . a sample taken from a vest-
pocket dictionary gives an estimated adult vocabulary of
11,700 words.

The fourth main source of misinformation stems from
the finding that a relatively small number of words accounts for most of the English language as it is used.

A fifth source of misinformation is the set of findings
from word counts of the speech of very young children
collected in either schools or home situations over a period
of a few weeks. . . . The common findings are that those
vocabularies do not exceed more than several thousand
words.

Having disproved all those fallacies, Seashore described in
detail his own method. He took the largest unabridged dictionary he could find, Funk and Wagnalls' two-volume set, and
devised an elaborate scheme to sample its contents. I can't
go into all his scientific safeguards here, but I can assure you
they were the outcome of many years of study and pilot experiments. The end result was the 24,000-word speaking and listening vocabulary among six-year-olds, rising grade by grade to
157,000 among college graduates.

Seashore concluded:

Much of our educational procedure is geared to pedes-
trian pace in vocabulary growth that is, at best, unrealistic,
and at worst, a hindrance, to all but the slowest of our
pupils. . . . We are actually holding back the progress
of our students by employing instructional methods and
materials which are based upon a limited vocabulary representing only a fraction of the potential learning abilities
of the students.

Naturally, the look-and-say Establishment didn't take all this lying down. There were two printed lengthy debates, one in which Dr. Seashore defended his findings against Professor E. W. Dolch, the inventor of the famous 200-word Dolch list of most frequently used words and a pillar of the look-and-say Establishment.

Professor Dolch's chief argument was that he'd asked "many parents" whether they thought their children learned ten new words a day. They thought it was ridiculous.

The next discussant was Dean J. C. Seegers, another pillar of the Establishment. He pulled some words like *degradation, sacrament, viceroy,* and *addiction* from the dictionary and asked Seashore whether he really believed his first graders knew those words. Seashore calmly referred to the principle of random sampling and referred to such words as *barking, quick, percolator, lead, pen, clear, pulse, cheer, weighty, falsehood, winged, cowardly, legal, kill, mouse, skill, aged, sea, blue,* and *gain,* which most people would agree that six-year-olds normally do know.

And so it went. The defenders of look-and-say fumed, but meanwhile other researchers followed Seashore's footsteps and came up with the *same findings.*

In 1947 Drs. Mary Schulman and Robert Havighurst did an experiment with eighth graders along the lines of Seashore's test. Their results were almost identical.

In 1951 Dr. Cynthia M. Colvin checked Seashore's figures on a group of seventh graders. The figures she came up with were much the same as Seashore's.

In 1952 Dr. Fred E. Bryan duplicated the Seashore experiment and came out with much the same figures except that he didn't test the first three grades orally and therefore didn't give them enough credit for the words they knew. But beyond those first three grades Bryan's estimates were almost as high as Seashore's.

In 1957 Dr. Mildred C. Templin again checked the Seashore findings. Her findings were slightly lower, but nowhere near the tiny vocabularies the look-and-sayers were working with. She also tested the difference in the scores of upper-socioeconomic and lower-socioeconomic children, but found it to be only 300 words, that is, a little over 1 percent.

Finally in 1959 there was a major study by Dr. Burleigh H. Shibles. He went over the whole ground once more, did a wholly fresh experiment, with monolingual and bilingual (French-Canadian) children in three schools in Maine, and arrived at findings that were even higher than those of Seashore's. His monolingual first-graders knew 26,363 words and even their bilingual classmates were not far behind with 17,847 English words.

And that's where the matter stands—or stood, you might say—until a very curious footnote in the book *Learning to Read: The Great Debate* by Professor Jeanne Chall, which I mentioned earlier in this book. The footnote read (page 203): "Estimates of the number of words first graders know vary from 2,000 to 25,000. See Lorge and Chall (1963) for a review of these studies and some of the methodological 'errors' that have resulted in the 25,000 figure."

In the text above the footnote, Professor Chall renders her own verdict: "The average first grader can probably use accurately and/or understand about 4,000 different words."

This is very strange. Professor Chall's book was written in the mid-sixties. At that time she was obviously acquainted with Seashore's famous, painstaking research as well as the fact that it had been confirmed by at least five independent researchers. How did she pare the "bombshell" figure of 24,000 down to an insignificant 4,000?

I could hardly restrain my curiosity about her astonishing feat until I got hold of the 1963 article with its "corrected" figures. Here's the story:

The article was called "Estimating the Size of Vocabularies of Children and Adults: An Analysis of Methodological Issues" by Irving Lorge and Jeanne S. Chall. (*Journal of Experimental Education*, vol. 32, pp. 147–157, 1963). Dr. Lorge died in 1961 and Professor Chall expressly took the responsibility for the study.

The computations of the article are extremely murky and it took me five readings to fully understand how Professor Chall arrived at her figures. For your benefit, I have converted everything into percentages of the original 24,000 words Seashore said a first grader is equipped with.

Now then. Professor Chall starts her work of downgrading

24,000 to 4,000 by pointing out that the original count contained names of persons, geographical place names, and word parts. "It is highly questionable," she says, "whether such words can be considered 'words' for estimating vocabulary knowledge." According to her count, these types of words add up to 30 percent of the original 24,000 words, that is, 7,200 words. Subtract them, and you're left with 16,800.

Now right away this seems utterly spurious. Why not credit the child with such words or word parts as Uncle Bill, Main Street, or "ex-" in "excuse"? What's the difference between those words and word parts and Uncle Sam, Chicago, and "con-" as in "confess"? "Highly questionable," I should say, Professor Chall.

But let's go on. The next category that Professor Chall questions is the "counting as different word forms several entries of the same word form . . . e.g. chest (of the body) and chest (of drawers)." Since Dr. Seashore explained at considerable length that he didn't do that, the new subtraction seems questionable on the part of Professor Chall. She figures 9 percent for that one. That deducts 2,160 from 16,800, leaving 14,640.

Next we come to duplicate spellings, accounting for 2 percent of Seashore's overall count. By this Professor Chall seems to mean words like *gage* and *gauge*. Well, all right, let's not quibble about that one. Two percent of 24,000 is 480, which leaves us with 14,160 words.

A word count of 14,160 words for six-year-olds at the beginning of first grade is still enormous in terms of look-and-say teaching and would leave the whole established system of reading nowhere. So a really radical method was still called for, and Professor Chall found it. Here's what she did.

She starts with the proposition that frequently used words are by definition easy, such as the words *how, so,* and *run.* Since such words take up extremely long entries in the dictionary, they give small children, Chall says, an enormous advantage since they are credited with a lot of those "easy" words under Dr. Seashore's sampling method. (He picked the third word on every other page.)

This sounds fine until you start to think what it means. The idea that frequent words are by definition easy stems directly from look-and-say teaching, where children are forced to memorize words until they come out of their ears. Therefore, a frequent word is an easy word—*for them*. But here we are dealing not with second- and third-grade victims of look-and-say but with preschoolers arriving at first grade, whose speaking and listening vocabulary is being estimated. They can't read and frequency of words means nothing to them. The words they easily remember are not *how, so,* and *run,* but words that stick in the memory once they're heard, like *elephant, Santa Claus,* or *fudge.* These are the words they add to their vocabularies regardless of their frequency.

My grandson Luke, now one and a half years old, heard the word *Valentine* naturally in the middle of February. He kept it stored in his memory until, sometime in April, he correctly identified a little drawing of a heart as a "valentine."

Similarly the researchers in Dr. George A. Miller's famous "kiddie lab" at Rockefeller University conducted a delightful experiment with the color *olive* and the word *chromium.* They casually dropped the word *chromium* (using it to mean olive-colored) into their conversation and waited for what would happen. Sure enough, their little three-year-olds began to use *chromium* for olive-colored as if this was the most natural thing in the world. (See Susan Carey's splendid article on "The Child as Word Learner.")

Based on the device of using word frequency, Professor Chall took another whopping 43 percent off Seashore's original 24,000 words, which left her with 3,800 words.

The rest was easy. There was a totally unexplained subtraction for "fauna and flora" (as if a child didn't know about dandelions or bunny rabbits). Grand result: Seashore's 24,000 words had been reduced to less than 4,000—a figure even the most timid look-and-say educator can live with.

Please note that this isn't just an amusing numbers game, but extremely serious. If a child knows only 4,000 words, there's some smidgen of a justification for teaching him 350 words a year to read. If he knows 24,000, the whole look-and-say system stands naked before the world as an out-and-out intolerable sham, a device to destroy the education of a great nation's children. Seashore knew what he was talking about. Now, forty years later, his voice has long been stilled and his name is almost forgotten.

On page 159 of his delightful book *Teaching to Read,* Mitford Mathews tells the following story:

A group of educators visited a Chicago parochial school where the Leonard Bloomfield phonic system was taught.

They were taken into a classroom of perhaps 40 first grade children. On the teacher's desk were elementary books from various grades. The visitors were invited to select a book and ask any of the children to read from it. The readiness with which the children read was unusual. One of the guests happened to pick up a sixth-grade science book and asked one of the boys to read a passage from it. In doing so the child encountered and read the word "satellite." Father Stoga (the superintendant) asked him what the word meant and the child said it meant a big object in the sky. Dean Gray, the man who gave us Dick and Jane, found the answer unsatisfactory, showing that the child was reading, that is pronouncing, quite beyond the vocabulary appropriate to his age, and not getting the sense of what he read. He explained to the other visitors that what the children were doing was in no sense remarkable. He said that reading experts had long known that children could rather quickly be taught to pronounce words with remarkable glibness but that real understanding of what was read was another matter entirely. He pointed out that these children were mere word-callers, that they were pronouncing well beyond their mental ages, and that they were heading straight for serious trouble later in their reading development.

11

"Your Child Isn't Ready"

Shortly after the appearance of my *Family Circle* article I got the following letter from a woman I'll call Maureen Bryant, who lives in upstate New York. She wrote:

Dear Dr. Flesch:

Thank you for writing the article "Why Johnny Still Can't Read" published in *Family Circle* (November 1, 1979). Your article confirmed my worst doubts about our own school system's method of teaching reading.

I had become increasingly suspicious of the method of reading being taught to my child at his elementary school. The school uses Scott Foresman and Co. texts exclusively. A child begins with Level 1 in the first grade and ends with Level 21 at the end of the sixth grade. So there are 21 books in their program; the completed worksheets brought home are taken from a set called *Reading Unlimited*.

Just as you explained in your article, a first grader is presented with words whose phonetic rules he has not been taught. Last October when my son was in the first grade, I questioned his teacher and expressed doubts about this method of reading. She told me not to worry; she said he would learn to read the words by sheer repetition.

This year he is in the second grade. He has been taken out of the school's main system of 21 levels because they say he did not do well on the test at the end of Level 4. They put him into a basic reading program by Scott, Foresman and Co. They say this program is "skills oriented" and they say it contains phonics work. He is now using what they say is a second grade reader called "Daisy Days." He will use only two books during the entire year of second grade. He will remain on "Daisy Days" until January.

Dr. Flesch, can you answer an important question for me? At the school I feel they do not welcome any questions nor do they answer them completely. Since I desire a phonics-first program, should I be happy now that my son is in the Scott Foresman and Co. basic reading program which includes "Daisy Days"? Is this a phonics-first program?

Thank you again for your wonderful article which explained how schools are robbing our children of the right to learn reading in the correct manner.

Yours truly,
Maureen Bryant

This is a classic case of the oldest of all alibis—the stall. Your child isn't doing so well in reading? Just wait a while—next year he'll do better. Meanwhile, we'll put him somewhere where he'll be busy for a while with easier books he won't have so much trouble with.

I answered Mrs. Bryant that *Daisy Days* was just as look-and-say as whatever Scott, Foresman books they'd given her poor boy before, and I recommended she should work with him on the exercises in my book *Why Johnny Can't Read*. She did so. He's now in the third grade and the best speller in his class. His early troubles are forgotten.

After all the research that has been done in the past twenty years on preschool and kindergarten reading, you may doubt that the now-antique concept of "reading readiness" is still alive and kicking. It most certainly is. At the slightest provocation it's being taken out of mothballs and thrown in the face of the poor mother who doesn't know any better.

The history of so-called reading readiness is, if possible, even funnier than the other Mickey Mouse research I've met on my safari through deepest Educatoria.

Back in 1931 the *Elementary School Journal* published an article by Mabel V. Morphett and Carleton Washburne, called "When Should Children Begin to Read?"

Washburne was then superintendent of schools at Winnetka, Illinois, an affluent suburb of Chicago. He was one of the most famous educators of his day. Miss Morphett was his research assistant.

The Winnetka schools were so high and mighty in those days that they didn't even use Dick and Jane or one of the other commercial basal readers, but their own Washburne-created system. It taught 37 sight words in the first semester of first grade and 102 other words in the second semester. (No phonics, of course.)

After the first semester the children were tested. Washburne tried to find what caused the reading difficulties of some of his Winnetka children. "In several instances," he wrote, "these children's mental ages on entering the first grade had been so low that discouragement had resulted from their first attempts to learn to read. This discouragement sometimes resulted in a mental set against reading which lasted for years and which hampered all their school work."

Reading this today, one can only admire the fine literary taste and good sense of those Winnetka first-graders of fifty years ago. They were not only "discouraged" by having to learn, through constant repetition, 37 inane little words—they were utterly disgusted, fed up to their teeth, bored to tears, and in a rebellious mood. In February, when the time for the first test came around, 25 of the 141 children said they didn't know the 37 words.

By the end of the year *all* 141 children had suddenly mastered the full 139 words and some had even memorized some second-grade words beyond the magic 139.

But Washburne had proven his point. Don't start to teach a child any sight words before his mental age is 6.5 (middle of first grade) or you are in for disaster, he concluded. For years afterward, he told the world, the children will be discouraged and set against reading.

For all I know, he may have been quite right. Children who aren't taught phonics from the start *are* discouraged and do develop a mental set against reading that lasts them a lifetime.

Anyway, the sacred Morphett-Washburne gospel held sway for about fifty years, and to this day children are declared "not ready" (like Mrs. Bryant's little boy) and sent back among the dummies until, with the passing of time, they've overcome their feeling of "discouragement."

Lots of things have happened since 1931 and all this seems like an old story. Reading has been discovered in kindergarten, in preschool day centers, and even in pre-preschool homes. Untrained laypersons of all kinds are teaching children the alphabet and, perish the thought, the sounds of the letters. The professionals, disturbed in their monopoly of teaching children over six and a half by the wretched look-and-say method, find themselves forced to fight a growing trend.

Dr. Louise Bates Ames, the spiritual heir of the Gesell Institute, fountainhead of reading delay, wrote in her 1966 book *Is Your Child in the Wrong Grade?*:

> We'd like to wait for beginning instruction in reading until the child is really ready. For some boys this age may well be eight *or even nine* years. Most reading failures and disabilities could be prevented if children were not started in reading till they were fully ready for such instruction.

By 1972, in her book *Stop School Failure*, Dr. Ames had come down one year:

> How long in general should you wait? It may be hard for you to believe, but there are some slow-developing boys who may not be ready to start reading till they are fully eight years of age. It's a long time to wait, but better to wait than start before they are ready, confuse them (often hopelessly), and then subject them to remedial reading instruction that may help temporarily but that may not be of lasting value. We repeat: *If you start teaching a child to read before he is ready, confusion and failure may very well result.*

By 1974 Dr. Ames had practically given up on her hopes of changing the American custom of starting school at six. In *Don't Push Your Preschooler* (written with Dr. Joan Ames Chase) she was content to accept the old Morphett-Washburne start-reading-at-six-and-a-half doctrine. Seeing parents all over the country letting their children read before entering school, she valiantly tried to stem the rising tide:

A child does not need to learn to read or write or count or even say his letters before he starts school in order to do a good job when he gets there. . . . Many a child will flourish in first grade and in the school years that follow even if there has been no emphasis whatever on academic subjects until the day that he begins first grade. . . . If you have no way of getting an evaluation of your child's maturity level, the chances are very good that if he or she is on the older side (fully five for girls, fully five-and-a-half for boys) before entering kindergarten, he will make it in school.

And then there's the book with the inimitable title *Predicting Reading Failure* by Drs. De Hirsch, Jansky, and Langford, which I mentioned before. They offer a test, rigged so that it almost invariably predicts "unreadiness." Then they blandly say: "We suggest, therefore, that the schools institute small transition classes between kindergarten and first grade for children who, regardless of age, are not 'ready.'"

Let's just postpone school another one-year period. *Then,* at last, they'll be ready for reading—by look-and-say, of course.

In the spring 1969 issue of the *Reading Research Quarterly,* Dr. Walter H. MacGinitie of Teachers College, Columbia University, at long last pointed his finger squarely at the shabbiness and intellectual dishonesty of the whole "readiness" argument.

Does the question *Is the child ready to begin to learn to read* make sense? It does only if precisely how reading will be taught has been specified [he wrote]. What would research on reading be like if it were guided by the question: *What and how is the child ready to learn?* . . . If the teaching method is not specified . . . the results may apply primarily to children taught by the unspecified method that was used.

Having clearly implied that the whole readiness business applies only to look-and-say and not to phonics-first, Dr. McGinitie has some mild academic fun with the book *Predicting Reading Failure:* "The question of how the children were taught to read was almost totally ignored. . . . This study asked *Is the child ready?* without explaining what the child had to be ready for."

In other words, "readiness" means that your child isn't ready for look-and-say until he or she is taught by that method in the middle of first grade by a properly accredited, thoroughly indoctrinated look-and-say teacher. Any attempt to teach a child by phonics-first is taboo, whether it's done in school or out of school, in kindergarten, in preschool, in the home, in special classes, or, heaven forbid, by misguided parents with the aid of unauthorized books, games, or other materials.

Professor Dolores Durkin, a pillar of the look-and-say Establishment, wrote in *Educational Leadership* of December 1978:

> Known words can be used to help children understand the alphabetic nature of our writing system. However, *only if children demonstrate the ability to understand and remember letter-sound relationships* should phonics instruction be pursued. To do otherwise is to foster negative attitudes toward reading and perhaps toward school itself.

A year before, in the September 1977 issue of *Young Children*, seven official organizations had warned against early phonics:

> A growing number of children are enrolled in pre-kindergarten and kindergarten classes in which highly structured pre-reading and reading programs are being used. ["Structured" is now the code word for phonics; it used to be "isolated skills."]
> In attempting to respond to pressures for high scores of widely used measures of achievement, teachers of young children sometimes feel compelled to use materials, methods, and activities designed for older children. In so doing, they may impede the development of intellectual functions such as curiosity, critical thinking, and creative expression, and, at the same time, promote negative attitudes toward reading.

This anti-phonics manifesto was signed by the following seven professional associations:

1. American Association of Elementary, Kindergarten, Nursery Educators
2. Association for Childhood Education International
3. Association for Supervision and Curriculum Development
4. International Reading Association
5. National Association for the Education of Young Children
6. National Association of Elementary School Principals
7. National Councils of Teachers of English

And now, at long last, I'll turn to the question of how very small children *do* learn to read.

The main source of information on this point is Professor Dolores Durkin's classic study *Children Who Read Early*, which she wrote in 1966.

The book is based on two intensive studies of children who entered first grade with a knowledge of reading. One was done in Oakland, California, in 1957 and the other in New York City in 1961. The Oakland early readers numbered 49, the New York City readers 156.

Professor Durkin found that her early readers learned from many different sources—mothers, fathers, older brothers and sisters, other helpers. A few of them apparently learned reading wholly by themselves—sometimes amazing their parents with their unsuspected knowledge.

There are about a dozen detailed case histories in the book, all of which are highly instructive. The children came from all kinds of backgrounds, rich and poor, educated and uneducated, black, white, and Oriental. Their ages ran from three to six, their IQs from low to high. There were about the same number of boys and girls.

Here's one of the case histories:

Little Angela, with a low IQ of 91 (9 points below the norm of 100) was black. Her father worked in a tire factory.

Her mother began to read aloud to her when she was two, always making sure that Angela could see the pages. Angela kept asking questions about the words on the page.

Angela missed the kindergarten cutoff age by only eight days, and for that reason her mother played "school at home" with her as a kind of consolation. She taught Angela the names of letters and colors and sometimes talked with her about the sounds of letters. For this, she followed the pages of a phonics workbook.

A second case history tells about Mark, a white New York City boy. He had an IQ of 115. His father was a businessman.

Mark taught himself from a few "teach yourself" workbooks. Most of them were about arithmetic but one was about phonics and one taught a child how to print. Mark's mother mentioned particularly his early interest in numbers. "He was the only child in kindergarten who could tell time," she said.

When the interviewer asked whether Mark's mother had given him any help with reading, she answered, "I tried to answer his questions." Later she said, "We sometimes talked about the sounds of letters. I was hoping he'd learn to figure out the words himself."

A third case history deals with Jack, a white boy with an IQ of 99. His father was an office manager. He was a great sports fan and talked a lot about sports to Jack, and the boy easily memorized batting averages, birthplaces, uniform numbers, and all kinds of other information.

Jack was "constantly scribbling," "terribly active," and "always had to be doing two or three things at a time."

Before he went to kindergarten, Jack watched a children's TV show every morning, but it was the weather, sports, and commercials that interested him most. When he was about four, he surprised his mother by reading some of the TV ads aloud.

At the end of her book, Professor Durkin summarized her findings.

1. Most of the early readers learned to print before they learned to read. They were "pencil and paper kids."
2. They constantly asked questions about spelling.
3. Their interest in writing and spelling led to interest in the sounds of letters.
4. Typically, those early scribblers and readers went through "interest binges." They followed those special interests over long periods and then suddenly dropped them. One mother said her daughter for many weeks

did nothing but copy people's names and addresses. Another mother's son had spent weeks making and remaking calendars.

Professor Durkin says nothing about phonics specifically, but the case histories again and again refer to questions about the sounds of letters, "sounding out," and the use of phonics workbooks. When Professor Durkin asked one of the children who had first taught her to read, little Carol's answer was "I think I did it by sounding out words myself."

Nowhere in Professor Durkin's book is there a single mention of a child who learned to read by anything resembling the look-and-say method—that is, by memorizing whole words, one after another.

Now let's look at a second group of remarkable children— those who, long before they could read, began to use "invented spelling." These children were first studied by Harvard psychologist Dr. Carol Chomsky, the wife of the famous language scholar Noam Chomsky. During the 1970s a number of scholars did more studies on the subject. They found that quite a few self-taught spellers could be found here and there, and that their madeup spelling devices were remarkably alike from Maine to California.

Those children, once they'd been taught the alphabet, began to use it ingeniously to express themselves in print. They used consonants the way they were usually sounded and made do for most vowels in one way or another. *H* was routinely used to express the sounds of *ch* or *tch; r* stood for *ar*, and so on.

One of Dr. Chomsky's five-year-olds, for example, wrote this invitation to a friend:

TAMMY I AM INVITIG U TO MI HAOOS TO HAV LUNTCH AND TO WOTCH SPEEDRASER NECXT WENSDA

A four-year-old wrote this get-well message:

2 DADDY I EM SRY TAT U R SIC NED LUV DADDY

A five-year-old wrote:

DER MUMOY I HOP YOO OR FEELIG BEDR I AM MKIG THS PRESIM FOOR YOO BI DIANE

One boy of five and one-half, confined to his room as a punishment, sent paper airplanes downstairs with these messages:

DADE I DONT LIK THIS ROOM WIN U GO UPSTERS
KEN I STA DAOON STERS
I AM CMIN DAOON STERS YES
I WIL KOMM DAOON STERS

Dr. Chomsky reported that these children are *not* unusually gifted or creative. All that's apparently needed is the kind of amused, indulgent parents who receive such messages without unduly worrying about their children's future spelling once they get to school. As a matter of fact, those children adapt very easily to orthodox English spelling. There's no report of any trouble in school.

In this connection, Dr. Chomsky quotes the famous Swiss psychologist Jean Piaget: "In order for a child to understand something, he must construct it himself, he must re-invent it. Every time we teach a child something, we keep him from inventing it himself."

In her comments, Dr. Chomsky also quotes the Italian educator Maria Montessori, who wrote: "Experience has taught me to distinguish clearly between *writing and reading,* and has shown me that the two acts *are not absolutely contemporaneous.* Contrary to the usually accepted idea, writing *precedes reading.*"

Montessori was opposed to many conventional ideas about teaching reading and habitually taught writing and reading—*in that order*—to children between four and six. There are now many Montessori nursery schools and kindergartens in this country. I think a knowledge of Montessori's work and views is essential for anyone who teaches children to read.

Maria Montessori was an Italian educator who lived from 1870 to 1952. She was the first Italian woman to get a medical doctor's degree. For a few years she taught feeble-minded children writing and reading until they could pass exams at regular schools. Then, in 1907, she turned to poor children between three and seven living in a Roman slum. A landlord had given her a room to take care of the children. Soon it turned out the children, who'd learned how to dress and undress, bathe themselves, put the room in order, and so on, wanted to learn

more. "A number of them came to us and frankly demanded
to be taught to read and write." They were joined by their
illiterate mothers.

Montessori decided to try. She prepared various materials
that would help the children learn, such as sandpaper letters
pasted on little wooden blocks and a "movable alphabet" made
of cloth.

After a few weeks of teaching the children with these phonic
tools there occurred a memorable scene in December 1907.
She describes it like this:

> One beautiful December day when the sun shone and
> the air was like spring, I went up on the roof with the
> children. They were playing freely about, and a number
> of them were gathered about me. I was sitting near a
> chimney, and said to a little five-year-old boy who sat
> beside me, "Draw me a picture of this chimney," giving
> him as I spoke a piece of chalk. He got down obediently
> and made a rough sketch of the chimney on the tiles
> which formed the floor of this roof terrace. As is my cus-
> tom with little children, I encouraged him, praising his
> work. The child looked at me, smiled, remained for a
> moment as if on the point of bursting into some joyous
> act, and then cried out, "I can write! I can write!" and
> kneeling down again he wrote on the pavement the word
> "hand." Then, full of enthusiasm, he wrote also "chim-
> ney," "roof." As he wrote he continued to cry out, "I
> can write! I know how to write!" His cries of joy brought
> the other children, who formed a circle about him, looking
> down at his work in stupefied amazement. Two or three
> of them said to me, trembling with excitement, "Give
> me the chalk. I can write, too." And indeed they began
> to write various words: *mama, hand, John, chimney, Ada*.
> The child who wrote a word for the first time was full
> of excited joy. He might be compared to the hen who
> has just laid an egg. Indeed, no one could escape from
> the noisy manifestations of the little one. He would call
> everyone to see, and if there were some who did not
> go, he ran to take hold of their clothes forcing them to
> come and see. We all had to go and stand about the written

word to admire the marvel, and to unite our exclamations of surprise with the joyous cries of the fortunate author. Usually, this first word was written on the floor and then the child knelt down before it in order to be nearer to his work and to contemplate it more closely.

After the first word, the children, with a kind of frenzied joy, continued to write everywhere. I saw children crowding about one another at the blackboard, and behind the little ones who were standing on the floor another line would form consisting of children mounted upon chairs, so that they might write above the heads of the little ones. In a fury at being thwarted, other children, in order to find a little place where they might write, overturned the chairs upon which their companions were mounted. Others ran toward the window shutters or the door, covering them with writing. In these first days we walked upon a carpet of written signs. Daily accounts showed us that the same thing was going on at home, and some of the mothers, in order to save their floors, and even the crust of their loaves upon which they found words written, made their children presents of *paper* and *pencil*. One of these children brought to me one day a little notebook entirely filled with writing, and the mother told me that the child had written all day long and all evening, and had gone to sleep in his bed with the paper and pencil in his hand.

After a short time all the children had learned to write. The next thing that happened was this:

Coming into the school one day, I found that the directress had allowed the children to take the tables and chairs out upon the terrace, and was having school in the open air. A number of little ones were playing in the sun, while others were seated in a circle about the tables containing the sandpaper letters and the movable alphabet.

A little apart sat the directress [Montessori avoided the word *teacher*] holding upon her lap a narrow box full of written slips, and all along the edge of her box were little hands, fishing for the beloved cards. "You may not believe me," said the directress, "but it is more than an hour since we began this, and they are not satisfied yet!" . . .

Seeing these surprising results, I had already thought of testing the children with print, and had suggested that the directress *print* the word under the written word upon a number of slips. But the children forestalled us! There was in the hall a calendar upon which many of the words were printed in clear type, while others were done in Gothic characters. In the mania for reading the children began to look at this calendar, and, to my inexpressible amazement, read not only the print, but the Gothic script.

From these casual beginnings in 1907 started the worldwide Montessori movement, with thousands of "children's houses" scattered through the world, where four- and five-year-olds are taught to write and read—always in this order. The now famous Montessori educational materials are still used and the children are always led to learn writing and reading by themselves and at their own pace.

In America the Montessori method was first opposed by the educators, but in the fifties there was a great comeback, and today there are thousands of Montessori schools all over the United States. They still follow, more or less, the original Montessori system. In a recent book, *Theories of Development* by William C. Crain, it is described like this:

First, the child is shown how to hold a pencil and then practices drawing by staying within outlines. . . . In another exercise, children trace their fingers over sandpaper letters which are pasted onto blocks of wood. . . . The letters are written in script rather than print because children find the movements of script freer and more natural. . . . They love repeating this exercise. . . . In a third exercise, children are given a movable alphabet which permits them to form the letters of words. For example, they look at a picture of a cat, sound out the letters and then make the word with the letters. This too they repeat endlessly, out of their spontaneous interest in the elements of spoken language. . . .

Through these and other separate exercises children learn the various skills involved in writing. When they finally put these skills together and begin to write letters, there usually follows an "explosion of writing." They will write all day long.

Writing paves the way to reading. Through writing, children form a muscular and visual memory of the letters and words and therefore can recognize them. Consequently, the five- or six-year-old who has learned to write can usually learn to read with very little help from the teacher. Children often say that nobody taught them to read at all.

During the entire preparatory period for writing and reading, the children do not even look at a book. Then, when they first pick up a book, they usually can begin reading it immediately. . . . There follows an "explosion of reading." Children delight in reading everything they see.

I visited a Montessori school a few miles from my home. I found everything as described. There were some twenty children in two large rooms, filled with stimulating things for them to work on. They drew, painted, built from blocks. Two little girls set the table for lunch, one of them meticulously counting out twenty-three paper cups for juice. Three four- or five-year-olds read for me with good intonation out of some children's book. One little girl laughed spontaneously at a funny passage. (I'd asked to have them read out of books they hadn't seen before.) One little boy handed me a crayon-colored flag of Uruguay, with "Uruguay" neatly spelled in crayon underneath.

I could hardly tear myself away from the place. The atmosphere was totally happy, all the children did what they wanted to do, no one was pushed to do anything.

The administrator told me I'd missed one of the famous "explosions" by just one day. The day before, a little boy had joyfully discovered how to tie shoelaces.

Since the Montessorians use no tests and don't publish statistics, the educators simply act as if such things don't exist. Most Montessori children enter school being able to read, but if they don't, nobody makes a fuss either. And so the two systems coexist. Twenty miles from the happy little Montessori school

I visited, there is New York City with millions of functional illiterates.

As if all this wasn't enough, the Montessori gospel contains another doctrine that is even more surprising. Maria Montessori not only taught millions of preschool children to read, but was firmly convinced that the age between four and six was the best time to do it. This is the famous Montessori theory of "sensitive periods." Learning begins with crawling, standing, walking, and so on, goes on to talking and, as I said, between four and six goes on to writing and reading. Teaching a child to write and read *after* that age, according to Montessori, is progressively harder.

This is not quite as eccentric as it may seem. The great philosopher Alfred North Whitehead wrote:

> It is not true that the easier subjects should precede the harder. On the contrary, some of the hardest must come first because nature so dictates, and because they are essential to life. The first intellectual task which confronts an infant is the acquirement of spoken language. What an appalling task, the correlation of meanings with sounds! It requires an analysis of ideas and an analysis of sounds. We all know that the infant does it, and that the miracle of his achievement is explicable. But so are all miracles, and yet to the wise they remain miracles. All I ask is that with this example staring us in the face we should cease talking nonsense about postponing the harder subjects.
>
> What is the next subject in the education of the infant minds? The acquirement of written language; that is to say, the correlation of sounds with shapes. Great heavens! Have our educationists gone mad? They are setting babbling mites of six years old to tasks which might daunt a sage after lifelong toil.

Once you start to think about it, the miracle of a very small child learning to speak his native language is so fantastic that teaching him to write and read immediately afterward makes a good deal of sense. The longer you postpone it, the harder it gets.

Montessori called these stages "sensitive periods," but the biologists, observing the same thing happening with animals, use the term "critical periods." The biologist Konrad Lorenz tells of a group of geese he kept separated from their parents immediately after birth. When they grew up, they never lost the habit of looking upon people rather than geese as their natural parents. By interfering during the "critical period" Lorenz had built the geese's attachment to people into their nervous system.

There is much research to be done in this area, but I wouldn't be at all surprised if Montessori was right and our current educational Establishment wrong. Four- and five-year-olds, far from being "unready" for reading, may be at exactly the right age for learning writing and reading quickly and painlessly.

12

"Your Child Is Disabled"

In February 1974 Dr. N. Dale Bryant, professor of psychology and education at Teachers College, Columbia University, wrote an article, "Learning Disabilities: A Report on the State of the Art." It appeared in the Columbia University *Teachers College Record*.

Dr. Bryant was and is a pillar of the educational Establishment. It was therefore downright sensational that he wrote the following: "It is possible that the [learning] disability is specific to the methods that have been used in teaching. Cases of reading disability in classes using the whole-word [look-and-say] approach might be different if the class had been taught with the phonetic or linguistic approach."

What! Was Dr. Bryant saying that learning disabilities may be the poisoned fruit of look-and-say teaching? The answer seems to be a clear yes. It is what most outstanding scholars in the field of reading are now agreed on. Before I follow Dr. Bryant's astonishing words with other, equally forceful quotations from his colleagues, let me explain what learning disabilities are and how the whole question arose.

Back in 1896, two English doctors, Dr. Pringle Morgan of Seaford and Dr. James Kerr of Bradford, independently discovered what seemed to be a brand-new disability, which they called "congenital word blindness." Dr. Morgan's patient was a fourteen-year-old bright schoolboy who wasn't able to read or write. Dr. Kerr's case was similar.

After these two pioneers, other doctors from Bohemia, Denmark, England, and America found similar cases. They apparently had discovered a new disease.

The term "congenital word blindness" gradually fell into

disuse, and the word "dyslexia" (bad speech) became the accepted term. (Some dozen or so other terms came and went, among them "perceptual handicap," "strephosymbolia," "specific language disability," "hyperactivity," "minimal brain damage," "minimal brain dysfunction," "developmental aphasia," and others.) In this book I'll use the term *dyslexia*.

If you're a general practitioner or pediatrician and a parent walks in with a child who has symptoms that point to dyslexia, you'll possibly look into the current edition of *The Merck Manual*, the most widely used annual reference book for physicians. There you'll find:

DYSLEXIA
(Congenital Word Blindness; Primary Reading Disability)

A condition in which an individual with normal vision is unable to interpret written language and therefore is unable to read. Educationally, the term is applied when a child of normal intelligence is two or more years behind his expected grade level in reading. A family history of language disorders is common, and boys are affected more often than are girls. The cause is unknown, but a CNS [Central Nervous System] defect in the ability to organize graphic symbols has been postulated. . . .

Symptoms and Signs
Dyslexic children are usually of normal or better intelligence. Their inability to read is inconsistent with their achievement in other school subjects, such as arithmetic. Spelling ability may or may not be impaired. Sensory deficits and neurologic impairment are absent. The child may be left-handed, right-handed, or ambidextrous, or dominance may be mixed.

Confusion in orientation of letters is the prime characteristic. This is manifested by reading from right to left, failure to see (and sometimes hear) similarities or differences in letters or words, or inability to work out the pronunciation of unfamiliar words. Attempts to read or write are characterized by letter and word reversals (e.g., "p" for "g," "saw" for "was") that are typical of normal 1st- and 2nd-graders, but persist in the dyslexic child. A

better-than-normal facility at mirror-reading or -writing
is common.

*In attempting to satisfy demands that he read, a dys-
lexic child may make up a story if the text contains a
picture or may substitute words for those he cannot read.
He may be able to vocalize words, i.e., to read aloud but
without comprehension.*

*Symptoms of frustration are inevitable. The reading
disability and its effects on learning and school performance may lead to behavioral problems, delinquency,
aggression, withdrawal, and alienation from other children, parents, and teachers.*

The language of *The Merck Manual* doesn't do justice to
the unbelievable oddity and variety of the symptoms of dyslexia. Not only can these unfortunate children neither write,
spell, nor read. They reverse words like *was* and *saw*, or *on*
and *no;* they can't tell right from left or up from down; they
can't remember words they memorized an hour ago; they can't
find their way to and from school; they mix up the sequence
of letters and spell *tight* as *tgiht* or *ihgt;* they do the same
with numbers and say that Columbus landed in 1924; they
mix up yesterday and tomorrow; they can't remember names
and faces; they have ordinary words like "pot" or "chair" at
the tip of their tongues but can't say them; their handwriting
is abominable; they're often clumsy and can't catch a ball; they
can't hold a pencil right; they are awful at jigsaw puzzles or
walking a chalkline.

They've been known to write "lunc," "Uncil Harry," "engen
repar shop," and they may spell measles "mealess," "misless"
or "measness."

A fourteen-year-old dyslexic boy could neither describe his
home nor remember whether his very blond brother had light
or dark hair. A fifty-year-old businessman wrote memos to his
secretary in mirror writing, which she then transcribed from
a mirror. Another middle-aged man slipped papers with the
names of new acquaintances into his pocket, so that he could
surreptitiously glance at them when necessary.

A bright ten-year-old dyslexic boy told his teacher he prefer-
red "tambourines to oranges because they are easier to peel."

Another said, "Although Columbus is given credit for discovering America, this is not necesselery so."

Dyslexic spelling goes way beyond ordinary misspellings. *Uncle* becomes "vlnt," *pocket* becomes "parr," *does* becomes "dev," *house* becomes "hemp," *not* becomes "mui."

Do I need to go on? There is a circus-freak quality about this disorder that makes it unbelievable unless you have actually seen and heard what it does to its unfortunate victims. (And, just to make things more confusing, not all dyslexics have all the symptoms.)

Needless to say, when the impairment was first discovered almost a hundred years ago, hardly anyone believed that such a thing could exist. The children were examined in all possible ways—their eyesight, their hearing, their intelligence (often superior)—but nothing was found. They carried some mysterious defect in their brains. Nothing seemed to help. Punishment didn't help; admonitions to try harder didn't help; tutoring didn't help. School year followed school year and the children got unhappier and unhappier, ridiculed, called "dumb" by schoolmates, isolated, punished for they knew not what crimes.

Then, in the early 1920s, a savior arrived on the scene in the person of Dr. Samuel T. Orton, a neuropsychiatrist from Iowa. Dr. Orton noticed some of those unhappy children in his travels from school to school. Pretty soon his fame spread and he became Professor of Neurology and Neuropathology at Columbia University in New York. In 1937 he wrote a book, *Reading, Writing and Speech Problems in Children*, which has since become the classic in the field.

Dr. Orton makes three important and hopeful points in his book:

1. True dyslexia is extremely rare.
2. Patients can almost always be helped and can learn to read and write normally, using a strictly phonetic teaching method.
3. Most patients are of superior intelligence and have excellent career potential.

And what does Dr. Orton say on the influence of the look-and-say method of teaching reading? Here it is (I quote from pages 175 and 176 of his book):

It may be noted that the methods recommended here are diametrically opposed to those which are currently in use in many schools. There has been in recent years a striking swing toward the use of the sight or flash-card method of teaching reading and away from the use of phonetics. The writer is not in a position to offer an opinion as to the efficacy of either of these methods as a general school procedure but their effect on children suffering from varying degrees of [dyslexia] has come under his immediate attention and he feels that there can be no doubt that the use of the popular flash method of teaching reading is a definite obstacle to children who suffer from any measure of this disability. We have no new numerical data to offer here since our work recently has dealt exclusively with referred cases and we have made no general surveys of the number of cases of the reading disabilities in schools using different methods. At an earlier period, however, some such surveys were undertaken in Iowa and they indicated strongly that where the sight or flash-card method of teaching reading was exclusively used, the number of reading disability cases was increased by three times that found in schools which used phonetic training for those children who did not rapidly progress by the flash-card method. As a further measure of the comparative efficiency of these two methods of teaching when dealing with a case of specific reading disability, it may be said that we have retrained a number of children who had not progressed beyond first grade reading skills after having spent three or four years in schools where the sight method was used exclusively, and have been able to advance them by two or more reading grades in one academic year by the application of the phonetic method. This has also been true in many cases in which the school program had been previously supplemented by intensive individual work but with no phonetic training or at best very inadequate attempts along these lines.

After Dr. Orton's death in 1948, the fame of what became known as the Orton-Gillingham method spread. (His assistant's name was Anna Gillingham.) There are now two basic books available, *Remedial Training for Children with Specific Disability in Reading, Spelling, and Penmanship* by Anna Gillingham and Bessie W. Stillman (1960) and *A Multi-Sensory Approach to Language Arts for Specific Language Disability Children* by Beth H. Slingerland (1971). The first is a general explanation of the Orton-Gillingham system; the second is a guide for primary teachers. Both are published by Educators Publishing Service, 75 Moulton Street, Cambridge, Mass. 02138.

The outstanding characteristic of the Orton-Gillingham system is that it works. It's based on a multisensory approach, teaching penmanship, spelling, and reading *together*. I don't mean to say that other phonic systems don't also work with dyslexics, but Orton-Gillingham is enormously thorough and unashamedly insists on endless drills.

As the number of dyslexics seemed to grow by the hundreds of thousands, word got around that Orton-Gillingham helped. In 1958 Miss Gillingham wrote a remarkable long letter to the editor of *Elementary English*. I quote:

Twenty years ago I was experimenting with the selection of kindergarten children who would probably have trouble with reading. . . . I shared the anxiety of many teachers and parents that being set apart in a special group would cast a stigma upon its members. However, we found our fears groundless. . . . Mothers came and asked for the privilege of having their children taught as a cousin or neighbor had been taught last year, "because he learned so much better.". . . Children asked "Miss Blank, am I going on this same way with you next year? It's a lot nicer than what the other children are having.". . . A third grade boy said, "Those kids learn a great deal that we don't know. We know a lot of words, but when we don't know a word we have to ask, and they can work it out for themselves.". . .

More and more emphatically it was forced upon my attention that there is no sharp line between the potential reading failure and the child who learns with a slight degree of success . . . It begins to appear that the alphabetic [phonic] approach may eventually come to be regarded as best for all.

Aside from this powerful word-of-mouth publicity, astonishing statistical data began to appear. Miss Margaret B. Rawson did a famous study following up the progress of dyslexic boys in the school in Rose Valley, Moylan, Pennsylvania, where she compared the progress of twenty normal boys with twenty others who'd entered the school as severe dyslexics and had been specially trained by Orton-Gillingham. After over twenty years they'd not only fully caught up with their unafflicted classmates, they'd reached excellent positions in life. Five were research scientists, two were physicians and two were college professors. Five others were teachers, three in high schools, one a full professor and department head at a large university and one of principal's rank and a member of the staff of a large-city superintendent. Five were business executives. One was an engineer and personnel manager for a large corporation. One was a lawyer. One was an actor with full-time employment in Hollywood.

There were plenty of other statistics and case histories. The outstanding success of the Orton-Gillingham method became simply a known fact; it was by far the most widely used method for the treatment of the ever-growing number of dyslexics.

And why had their number grown so enormously? More and more reading researchers thought they'd found the obvious answer.

In 1966 Dr. Leon Eisenberg wrote: "The potentially dyslexic child may have his disability magnified by exclusive reliance on the whole word method."

In 1970 Dr. S. Jay Samuels wrote: "A reading disability is said to exist when despite adequate instruction . . . there is a discrepancy between the child's reading achievement level and measure of potential ability. . . . It is difficult to understand how we can consider instruction to be adequate in the face of the grim facts about reading deficiencies provided by the Office of Education."

In 1971 Dr. Bruce Balow wrote: "In recent years there has been a great tendency to attribute special learning disabilities to a number of youngsters whose difficulties are not very special, not very specific, and not very clearly related to neurological deficiencies. . . . If the problem can be defined out of education into the realm of medicine, educators can then remain relatively complacent about their efforts to correct the problem. With such a medical excuse, it is possible to ignore the educational limbo to which most such children are consigned."

In 1973 Dr. S. Alan Cohen wrote: "Some day, pedagogy in general may be as good as it could be. . . . At that time, most children with or without neurological symptoms will be reading adequately."

In 1974 Dr. N. Dale Bryant wrote the words quoted at the beginning of this chapter.

Again in 1974 Dr. Barbara Bateman wrote: "Many would exclude from the category of learning disabled those children who have not had adequate reading instruction. The assumption that instruction is adequate is probably false when it is made regarding conventional whole-word, meaning-emphasis instruction. . . . Learning disabled children are those who must be taught by the best reading methods available if they are to succeed. As taught, they can and do learn to read. . . . Therefore, *teaching disabilities* is a more precise term than *learning disabilities* for the cause of reading failure."

In 1975 Dr. Hugh W. Glenn wrote: "To say that a child is learning disabled is simply a way of saying that he . . . needs instruction by an insightful teacher who uses current information on how language works and how children learn. The child does not need someone who pins a label on him to give his teacher a reason for failing him."

Again in 1975 Dr. Richard L. Allington wrote: "By assigning a label educators attempt to shift the responsibility from teacher to learner. If one assigns a child a label, the implication exists that there is an inherent lack in that child. That is, no teacher would be criticized for not teaching a dyslexic to read. What we are faced with is not a child who is lacking, but a teacher or school that is lacking."

In 1976 Dr. Cecelia Pollack wrote: "After more than a decade of analyzing children's learning difficulties, we are forced to look to the role of the schools as an important causative factor."

In 1977 Dr. Frank R. Vellutino wrote: "There is now considerable evidence which questions earlier suggestions that reading disability may be intrinsically associated with phonological deficiencies resulting only from dysfunction in auditory discrimination. An alternative possibility is that many children have not become aware of the phonetic structure of both spoken and printed language."

Also in 1977, Dr. Carl L. Kline wrote: "The existing school system is irrational, ineffectual, authoritarian, inept, smug, defensive, and undereducated. I suspect that ineffective teaching and poor methodology cause about 90 percent of the reading disabilities in our schools."

And in 1979 I met Mr. Siegfried Engelmann and asked him what he thought about dyslexia. "Dyslexia?" he answered. "I call it *dysteachia.*"

So here are twelve outstanding scholars in the reading field firmly convinced that dyslexia is not a rare disease but simply the outcome of look-and-say teaching. Can this be true? For the answer I went to the works of Dr. Wilder Penfield, the world-famous Canadian brain expert, to find out exactly how the brain works during the process of reading, writing, and remembering. Dr. Penfield, in his book *The Mystery of the Mind,* says that every impression on the mind leaves a memory trace—or "engram"—that may be strong or weak, depending on the amount of attention we give it. When we remember, we activate the engram. The stronger it is, the better the memory and the more we have learned. "The imprint of memory's engram," Penfield wrote, "is somehow added during neuronal action. Conscious attention seems to give to that passage of neuronal impulses permanent facilitation for subsequent passage of potentials along the neuronal connections in the same pattern. Thus, a recall engram is established. This, one may suggest, is the real secret of learning."

When the child reads a word like *cat,* the three letters *c-a-t,* in this sequence, are associated with the sound of the word and its meaning, and form an engram in the brain. If the child's engram-forming capacity is weak—because of a tendency toward dyslexia—the engram will be weak. Next time he sees the word *cat,* it may remind him of nothing, or he will read it *atc* or *tac* or whatever. He may pronounce it in all kinds of ways. He may remember absolutely nothing of its meaning or mix it up with *dog* or *cop* or *red.*

But, I said to myself in my medical ignorance, does all this mean that look-and-say teaching can *produce* dyslexia? Can a misguided teaching method cause a national epidemic? True enough, the dyslexically inclined child sees the picture of a cow and the word *cow* underneath. If he's been taught phonically, he'll read, in left-to-right order, the sounds of *k* and *ow* and there'll be no problem. But if he's being taught by look-and-say, he may read the word from right to left, or he might read the beginning *c* and vaguely remember the picture of the cow, or he might see some "global" bundle of *c, o,* and *w* and establish a weak, confused connection with a four-footed animal—say, a large dog or a goat. Who knows how look-and-say teaching will affect a child's brain? One thing is certain. He will form some sort of an engram, and next time he sees the word *cow,* this engram will, in Dr. Penfield's words, "be facilitated" and he'll make the same sort of mistake again. And again, and again, and again, up to third grade, and eighth grade, and college—if he ever gets there.

I couldn't quite believe in this "epidemic" idea and went to consult my good friend Dr. Hilde Mosse, Associate Professor of Psychiatry at New York Medical College and for many years school psychiatrist of the New York City Board of Education. Dr. Mosse is one of the foremost national authorities on reading disorders and has just written a new book about them.

My simple question and Dr. Mosse's answer turned into a profound discussion that lasted several hours.

"Is it possible that the look-and-say method is responsible for a national epidemic of dyslexia?" I asked.

Dr. Mosse fell into a long silence.

"First of all," she finally said, "the simple answer to your question is no. There's no such thing. No system of training, however bad it may be, can produce an impairment or disorder of the brain. By the way, I don't like to use the word 'disease' in the case of dyslexia. It *isn't* a disease, something that invades the body at a given moment. Rather I'd like to call it an impairment or a disorder. You said 'weakness' a while ago. That's a good word. It's a weakness of a child's memory and perception, localized in the area where the brain deals with reading, listening, language, and all that.

"Now the look-and-say method can't create such an impairment where it doesn't exist—even if there is a basic tendency.

"But the constant barrage with those wrongly formed engrams and the continuing strengthening and 'facilitation' can and do have a similar effect. The whole-word method doesn't *produce* the disorder, but it does a marvelous job of aping its symptoms—the uncertainty about the direction of letters and about their sounds, the trouble with blending, the uncertainty about the sequence of letters within words, the guessing of words from their beginning consonants, the invention of words or sentences with no relation to the text.

"The same dyslexia-like symptoms appear in writing to dictation or self-composed writing.

"So look-and-say can't give a child dyslexia, but it can and does give a splendid imitation of it."

"Wonderful," I said. "I think you've got it exactly. But now comes the all-important point. How can you tell? What do you do to find out whether a patient has true dyslexia or is just a victim of look-and-say?"

Again Dr. Mosse thought long and hard.

"First I always give them a test. Any one of the regular reading tests will do. If the child knows phonics, he'll try to puzzle out and sound out an unfamiliar word and behave like someone who is familiar with the alphabetic-phonic principle. You can see this in a minute. If a phonically trained child has a reading problem, then you have to examine him thoroughly, find out what's at the bottom of it—perhaps he's emotionally disturbed, perhaps it's one of a million other things—and you have to treat him, hoping that in time he'll respond.

"But if the child knows *nothing* about phonics—and the vast majority falls into that group—the job is very much easier. He's probably not a true dyslexic, but simply one of the thousands and thousands of victims of look-and-say. He must be taught phonics."

I still wasn't fully satisfied. "If, as you say, the true dyslexic has to be taught phonics and the almost indistinguishable look-and-say-taught child must *also* be taught phonics, where do you draw the line? What's the difference between the two?"

Again there was a long pause. "You'll just have to wait," my medical oracle finally said. "If it's just a simple case of look-and-say misteaching, it won't take too long. Sooner or later—hopefully sooner—the child will catch on. He'll suddenly understand the phonetic principle—I've seen this happen hundreds of times right in this office. And then, in a reasonably short time, he'll learn. His 'disease' will be cured—or at least vastly improved. Spelling improvement is by far the hardest job, and many people will stay poor spellers all their lives.

"But the true dyslexic is different. These cases are very rare, but since I am a psychiatrist specializing in these matters, I have seen quite a large number. They're referred to me, you see.

"The difference between a true dyslexic and a look-and-say victim is simply a question of time. With a true dyslexic you have to work and drill and exercise for months and months— sometimes two or three years. They all eventually learn to read and write, but it takes an awfully long time—plus a lot of patience, plus strong motivation. It can be done, with excellent results. I cannot remember a single case that didn't respond."

What exactly is the famous Orton-Gillingham method? It is a kind of super-careful, super-patient, super-relentless phonics. In 1966 Dr. Orton's widow gave a lecture describing his approach:

Start with the teaching of the basic letters and sounds. Show how they are related. Always teach speaking, listening, reading, and writing at the same time. Carefully, step by step, teach the shorter sequences, then the longer sequences, the letter-sound patterns, sequences of two or more syllables, and words in phrases and sentences. "When the pupil has thoroughly mastered these cumulative skills, he will be able to recognize many words almost at sight with full awareness of their meaning— he will, in fact, have learned how to read."

(Yes, it's all the same, reinvented three or four times—the Gagné task analysis and subskill approach, the Montessori sequence of materials, the Orton step-by-step approach—there's nothing new anywhere, only an unbelievable history of denials and coverups.)

"Our approach," Orton wrote, "has been an attempt to capitalize upon children's auditory competence by teaching them the phonetic equivalents of the printed letters and the process of blending sequences of such equivalents so that they might produce for themselves the spoken form of the word from its graphic counterpart."

And in 1946 he added: "Whether or not our theory is right, I do not know, but I do know that the methods of retraining which we have derived from that viewpoint have worked."

They certainly have. I mentioned the seemingly endless stock of statistics and case histories the Orton-Gillingham people have assembled. Here, to illustrate the difference between true dyslexia and what I'll call "look-and-say disease," I'll retell only four of those case histories—two of true dyslexia and two of the "look-and-say" imitation.

In the February 1973 issue of *McCall's*, Mr. Kenneth L. Woodward told the story of his older son, who suffered from dyslexia. Throughout kindergarten, first and second grade, the boy did fine, but at the beginning of third grade the trouble started. His grades dropped to Bs and Cs. The school psychologist pronounced him a mild dyslexic, he stopped doing his homework, he was moody and unhappy. The Woodwards took the boy to their pediatrician, who in turn sent them to Dr. Katrina De Hirsch, the famous New York City expert in learning disabilities.

Dr. De Hirsch found the boy couldn't discriminate easily between certain sounds. He showed signs of "mixed dominance." No wonder he was emotionally disturbed. "You have a bright boy," she told the unhappy parents, "but he has a brain dysfunction that will affect his ability to learn the rest of his life."

Luckily, the Woodwards found an Orton-Gillingham disciple near their home in Ossining, New York. She was Mrs. Nina Traub, a renowned teacher of learning-disabled children. She turned the boy over to one of her students, who tutored him for eighteen months, using Mrs. Traub's book, *Recipe for Reading*—a somewhat simplified offspring of Orton-Gillingham.

After one-and-a-half years young Woodward was up to par in his reading and writing, and happiness returned to the Woodward household. I talked to his father recently and he told me his son, now at college, is doing splendidly.

The next story has a happy outcome, but there was a long, unhappy detour. It's an autobiographical account from *Developmental Dyslexia* by Dr. Drake Duane and Paula Dozier Rome. Forty-year-old "David" writes:

The first time I can remember being conscious of having a reading problem was when I was in the second grade. I was having trouble with reading, and they put me into a special reading school.

. . . Every class was just a struggle if anything about reading was involved. My grades were never good. The biggest thing I remember about grade school is the frustration. In high school I sometimes could get around the different subjects by taking my studies home and working extra hard, but I still never got very good grades. I found I could avoid very painful types of experiences by getting into activities that didn't require reading. For example, I took auto mechanics just as soon as I got into high school and was able to choose electives.

. . . This sort of thing happened to me all the time. I would take up things that wouldn't involve reading and learn that I was very good at them. It was a way to avoid reading, a way to avoid the pain of feeling stupid, of being dumb, of not being able to read or write. I took up athletics, and I took up woodworking. I would get As in woodworking, but in anything that had to do with reading it was either a D or I was right on the line of failing.

. . . I went on to junior college and was taking English and orientation and lots of other courses. I had a hard time of it. . . .

. . . I had a chance to go into the printing business and became a photolithographer. That didn't require a lot of reading. I went into color separation and plate making, stripping, and other things that didn't require reading. I would have to read to get the technical knowledge required to do the job, but I avoided jobs that would require other types of reading. Eventually I became a department head.

. . . I knew that I was a problem solver and that I could usually solve any problem that came up. Other people, who were in a higher position than I was, would have to rely on me.

Sometimes I would start talking about one of these problems, and the other fellow would say, "Why don't you write that down?" I had one instance like that in the micro-research program. We had a problem and several possible solutions. The manager said, "Write these on the board for me." I got up and went over to the board, and as soon as I got there I couldn't write the slightest word. I couldn't even write the word "the." My mind went blank, and I just could see the feeling that "Hey, if you can't read and write, you've got to be ignorant."

I decided at that point that this was not the type of life I would like to lead. It was then that I found out about dyslexia. I was referred to a reading center [and taught by the Orton-Gillingham method]. . . .

. . . Once I began to understand my problem, I began learning things I never thought I would be able to pick up. Now I am able to pick out a word that I have never seen before and sound it out. It was a kind of revelation to me.

I have gone back to college. I am carrying a 3.5 or 3.6 average, and I am just elated. The subjects are fantastic. I am taking a mass-communications course and classes in English.

. . . Right now I am trying to achieve a career level that I feel is equal to my abilities. It is difficult. I know there are people in management who have much less capability than I do, but I am still on the level of a technician because of my problems in reading and writing. These problems have stereotyped me into being the dummy.

Both young Mr. Woodward and "David" were true dyslexics—the real, rare, puzzling, inexplicable kind. My next two examples were imitation patients—simple, garden-variety victims of common American look-and-say.

Here's the first case. It comes from a letter from Mrs. Kathryn Diehl, former research director of the Reading Reform Foundation and a woman with long experience in tutoring children with reading troubles. She writes:

Although most children simply can't memorize many sight words and often are confused by similar-looking words, there are some who can memorize a few thousand

and keep them straight. They're called the "good readers" at school.

But at some point sight readers reach books with too many unknown words and their actual illiteracy shows up at last. The most fascinating example I remember was a junior high school boy I'll call Richard.

Richard was fourteen years old and a military officer's son who had moved all over the country in his elementary school years. He evidently had had nearly every widely used basal reading series in the different schools he attended. As those series don't use many of the same words, transferring from one district to another often brings early open failure.

But Richard was different. He was the only child I have ever seen who had been able to learn many thousands of sight words perfectly by the memorization and repetition methods in the conventional basal series. He had learned all the words in all the readers in the schools he attended and had received A and B grades through elementary school years. He was considered an excellent reader.

In junior high, this false image collapsed. He couldn't read the secondary-level textbooks with larger vocabulary and his grades fell to D and F in all academic subjects, although he was a very nice, well-behaved boy who tried to do well. This was ten years ago. Today they have cut down the vocabulary in the junior and senior high school textbooks to enable more of the students to read them. Now, Richard's actual functional illiteracy probably wouldn't become obvious until he reached high school or even college.

I found out in the first few minutes of the first hour I tutored him that it would be impossible to teach him in the customary way. He could read any simple material limited to common words very fluently, with his instant recall of that huge store of sight words. He knew most of the consonant sounds but his knowledge of the vowel sounds was very skimpy. And he had never been taught how to sound out words, of course, so the letter sounds he did know were the useless and unused knowledge they are to millions of students taught with the sight word theory programs.

Right in front of his parents and teachers all along—unrecognized—had been the visible proof that he really was almost illiterate: his spelling and writing ability were very poor. His spelling of many common little words was terrible. Nor can a child write anything worth reading when limited to the "most common words," with no ability to use any of the hundreds of thousands of other words in the English language.

To the initiated, other strong evidence that he really was a very poor reader would have been the fact that he never had read a book for pleasure outside school in spite of his "success" during his elementary years. However, parents usually assume their children just don't like to read. They don't realize that library books have so many unknown words that children "don't like to read" because all the interesting books with good vocabulary are too hard for them.

The only way to teach him to use letter sounds was to teach him to spell the easy common words he already could read very well. Of course there were thousands of simply spelled less-common words he couldn't read, but there was no time to determine them and write special practice reading material using them. His mother was bringing him here on Saturdays from out of town, a 40-mile round trip. She and his St. Bernard dog were waiting outside in the car during his lessons and both of them would rather have been elsewhere.

The lessons consisted mostly of spelling dictation, using the reading vocabulary lists from a first grade real phonics reading system, which introduces one new letter sound spelling at a time for practice. He took pride in showing how rapidly he could write the words as I dictated the lists to him, and soon was making few mistakes.

He learned the letter sounds and how to use them to read new words, also, so easily that he soon made a game of trying to fool me. He would read aloud a word list or paragraph at top speed, and then ask me: "Which words did I have to sound out to be able to read them?" This so quickly became lightning-like ability that very soon I couldn't tell which ones had been unfamiliar new words to him. It appealed to his sense of humor to have me guess wrong and to explain my mistakes soberly but eyes twinkling.

He learned to read independently in five hours. He learned the entire phonics system so fast that by the fourth lesson we were hunting for reading material with difficult polysyllabic words for him to practice on. Simple words quickly had become no challenge to him. This was solved by reading articles in adult news magazines, choosing the subjects he wanted to read about.

After five lessons his mother called to tell me that his new report card showed he had jumped from Ds and Fs up to As and Bs in all his subjects. Now he could read his 8th grade textbooks and anything else he wanted to.

We canceled the course.

My fourth and final story comes from Dr. Linda Meyer, professor of educational psychology at the University of Illinois. It's the story of her younger brother Fred. I'm glad it also has a happy ending, but unfortunately that's not typical. Typically, there's tragedy at the end for millions of children like Fred.

Fred entered first grade in a small Midwestern town in September of 1952. He was young for his grade, but noticeably bright. He had walked and talked early. He had well-developed social skills. He was the first son in a family of two children. I was just a year and a half older. No problems had been evident in kindergarten, but Fred developed reading difficulties almost as soon as reading instruction was begun in first grade. The Scott, Foresman basal was the text for the class, and his first grade teacher followed it to the letter. Fred now describes those early lessons as providing him with a total lack of understanding about how to identify words. He was confused, he was constantly worried that he would be called upon to read. He omitted words, misidentified words, left off endings, added endings, and generally made many mistakes.

His problems continued throughout first grade, though

he received passing marks. Our parents were not alerted to his problems, though they sensed that Fred was becoming increasingly nervous. They were informed that Fred was becoming a "behavior problem." His teacher commented that he enjoyed talking with classmates and while he generally got along well socially, he was often out of seat, or was busying himself with activities that were not school-related.

During Fred's second grade year, our family moved to a new school district. Fred was placed in a rural school, in which first, second, and third grades were taught by one teacher. Fourth, fifth, and sixth grades were taught by a second teacher. The classes were very small, and teachers worked with entire "classes" at one time for all academic instruction, though tutoring or special work was often accomplished by combining students from different grades. Shortly after the move, our parents were summoned to school. They were informed that their son would be retained in second grade. His reading was poor. He could not figure out new words. He had no knowledge of the sounds of letters, and he could not spell. In addition, he was acknowledged to be "immature." While our parents had some idea that problems had been brewing, they were not prepared for this news.

They developed a plan. The first step was to have a complete battery of psychological tests administered. These tests showed that Fred was considerably above average in intelligence, and apparently well adjusted socially. There were no apparent reasons for his failure to learn to read. Our parents were greatly relieved and rationalized that after all, Fred was young, and repeating second grade would probably be good for him. They still had no idea that it would be necessary to provide instruction that would teach him how to decode words.

Fred's problems increased. He was a failure in school. He was embarrassed when asked to read. Because there were three classes in the same room, first and third graders could listen as the second graders read. He began to think of himself as a failure, and he began to stop trying in school. While he continued to enjoy school socially, he sensed that teachers liked "good" students. Because he was not a good student, he felt as if teachers were constantly against him, and he turned off learning. He spent his time in other ways.

He repeated second grade. He went through third, fourth, and fifth grades before attempts were made to provide help outside school. The fourth and fifth grade teacher had been particularly rough on Fred, and she was considering holding him back a second time. This time, our parents decided to take action. They talked to the teacher that Fred would have in sixth grade and arranged to have him tutored. At the same time, Fred's new teacher recognized the problem and started helping him herself. She sensed that most of Fred's problems in math were related to his problems in reading. He could not read the math problems well enough to work them correctly. By fifth grade, Fred's reading problems were causing serious problems in other subject areas.

Tutoring began in the summer, and it continued through the school year. The teacher taught Fred sounds, and how to sound words out. She provided several books and stories that were interesting and fun. She also taught sentence diagramming as a way of identifying words and the functions of the words. She treated Fred with warmth and kindness. He liked her. She liked him. They looked forward to their time together, and Fred's reading improved. His attitude toward school also improved. By the time school started, Fred was looking forward to it in ways that he hadn't for several years. His most difficult times with reading seemed to be over, but his problems with spelling and self-concept continued. By Junior High, Fred was recognized as a very bright student who had terrible spelling habits. Spelling is still a problem, and Fred, who is now 33, thinks that it took him until college to overcome the fears of failure that he had lived with for so many years. In fact, by his senior year in college, he carried more hours than a business student had carried before at the University, and he made the Dean's list. He went on to earn a Master's Degree in Labor and Industrial Relations, and has been extremely successful as an organizer of professional people.

This story has a happy ending. The happy ending is the result of time and effort that concerned parents gave to work with a son who was obviously bright, but who had been taught to read with a sight reading program. The most serious aspect of the story is the effect that the first two years of school had on Fred. His failure devastated him, turned him off learning, and made him feel that he wasn't capable of learning. That's a terrible thing to do to a child . . . to allow them to fail *before* putting them into a program that will teach them effectively. How much better to start all children out in programs that will prevent failure. That's what Fred and his wife plan to do. They will teach their children to read with phonics before the children are ready for school. They won't run the risk of having a child fail.

How many of these stories could be prevented? How many more children can be taught to read without trauma from failure?

You'll ask, rightfully, what the educational Establishment did in the face of such overwhelming successes of phonics-first to hide or distort what was happening.

Well, they did the usual thing. First of all they spread the usual type of confusion. In an article, "Orton Revisited" in the December 1974 *Reading Teacher*, Professor Ilva T. Schweizer sums it up:

> What, then, may we conclude? Does success lie in any particular method? Not likely. Innumerable methods have flowered and died, and bloomed again. "So many instructional methods have been tried, and so many succeed (in some instances, at least) that further permutations in the game of instructional roulette are unlikely to produce any great gain, either by chance or design."

(The quotation is by Professor Frank Smith of "psycholinguistics" fame.)

The next step in the by now so hackneyed coverup procedure was the invention of all kinds of nonsense that was supposed to do the job better than phonics.

The prize item in this respect was the famous Marianne Frostig system, which enjoyed a tremendous vogue in the fifties and sixties. Mrs. Frostig didn't teach reading—she applied her own brand of perceptual therapy.

There were many other "perceptual" trainers. They did all kinds of things except teaching a child to read.

In a review article by Nancy C. and Robert K. Hartman in *The Reading Teacher* (April 1973), the process is described as follows: First the learning-disabilities specialist gives the child a large number of tests. Then he or she declares that the child has a visual perceptual handicap:

> Her recommendation then is centered on attempting to *correct this defective process* of visual perception. She assumes that this process is the cause of the reading difficulty and, therefore, the reading itself cannot be significantly improved until the defective process itself is improved. Her program of remediation may include exercises such as those provided by the Frostig Program or . . . visual tracking and convergence exercises. . . . More extreme examples of perceptual training programs may have the child walking balancing beams . . . or jumping on trampolines. . . . The most extreme case is that of Delacato whereby the child is taken through the developmental steps of creeping, crawling, and other patterning exercises.

I quote from Professor Carl H. Delacato's book, *The Treatment and Prevention of Reading Problems,* page 84:

> Boy A's sleeping position was changed to a posturalized position, wherein he slept with the right arm flexed, his face facing his right thumb, his right knee flexed, and his left leg and left arm extended. He was not allowed to attend music classes at school and was not allowed to listen to music at home during the six-week pre-remedial period.

The Hartmans reviewed the work of seventeen—seventeen!—researchers who had to spend untold hours, months, and years of their lives, plus countless amounts of grant money, to disprove all that nonsense. Of course the perceptual training and the balance-beam walking and the trampoline jumping and the sleeping turned to the right thumb and the total abstention from disco or Bach didn't teach children to read. The seventeenth researcher, Dr. C. L. Rosen, concluded mildly, "The gains as a result of the perceptual training did not seem to transfer to the academic task of reading."

After these activities had failed to displace the Orton-Gillingham approach, there was a brief interlude of giving the kids pills against "hyperactivity." But nobody ever pretended that Ritalin, Cylert, or any of the other pills ever taught a single child to read. Then the educators hit upon an entirely new idea. They'd rename dyslexia out of existence.

In 1963 Professor Samuel Kirk used in a speech the term "specific learning disabilities" and somehow the term stuck. It is now embodied in Public Law 94–142, the federal law that deals with the education of the handicapped. The definition is published at 42 Federal Register 65081 (December 29, 1977). It reads:

> "Specific learning disability" means a disorder in one or more of the basic psychological processes involved in understanding or in using language, spoken or written, which may manifest itself in an imperfect ability to listen, think, speak, read, write, spell, or to do mathematical calculations. The term includes such conditions as perceptual handicaps, brain injury, minimal brain dysfunction, dyslexia, and developmental aphasia. The term does not include children who have learning problems which are primarily the result of visual, hearing, or motor handicaps, of mental retardation, of emotional disturbance, or of environmental, cultural or economic disadvantage.

As you can see, "specific learning disabilities" are all those that aren't paid for by the federal government under any other existing law. They must not be more than two percent of the total federal funds paid to a school for educational help.

You notice that the term covers all those old terms that called for a specific diagnosis, like "dyslexia," "perceptual handicaps," "minimal brain dysfunction," and so on. "Specific learning disabilities" is about as soothing as you can get if you have to tell a couple of worried parents that their child is sick.

So the term took hold. On the basis of "learning disabilities" (or "L.D." for short) schools can now get up to two percent of their money for handicapped children from the federal government.

And, as you see, the definition is wide as a barn door and wholly negative. If the child doesn't get any federal money on other grounds, the school can always say he can't read because of some mysterious ailment. If it isn't Dr. Orton's "strephosymbolia," let's call it "chronic truancy" or "book phobia" or whatever. The main thing is it is never the school's or the method's fault, but the fault of the poor victim.

True dyslexia, that forgotten rare disease, has now totally gone out of style. In a popular textbook, *Reading Disability* by Florence G. Roswell and Gladys Natchez, reading improvement now takes a backseat.

> We do not focus so much on "success" in reading per se [the authors write]. In our society there is enough pressure for that. We try to mitigate such pressures by emphasizing the way the child reacts to his predicament. Perhaps he can accept the fact that he is not near the "top" of his class. He may even come to understand that being on top is precarious too—one can so easily be toppled. We encourage him to make his own contribution in his own way and to accept himself as much as possible. (Page 76.)

In keeping with this philosophy the phonic method is reduced to 7 pages of the 306-page book.

But even that is not the ultimate in leaving the poor nonreader to his own devices and telling him to be happy with his lot. The parents have to be pacified too.

In a recent contribution to this vast literature, *Learning Disabilities—A Family Affair* by Betty Osman, a fictitious, typical case of "Teddy" is discussed. "How far Teddy will go in a straight academic curriculum remains to be seen." (Nowhere, obviously.)

His guidance counselor and his parents are searching for an area of strength that could be pursued during the rest of his school years. . . . Recently his parents and I recalled that he had always shown a keen interest in his mother's vegetable garden and houseplants. Perhaps horticulture and landscape gardening might provide an interesting future career for him to consider.

(Let him go to his grave as a nonreader, being paid minimum wages for backbreaking labor.)

Mrs. Osman is a graduate of Vassar College and Teachers College, Columbia University. She is an adjunct professor at Manhattanville College in Westchester County, New York, and runs a private practice as a specialist in learning disabilities.

In her book the term "learning disabilities" is hardly ever mentioned. She prefers the most soothing and innocuous term of them all—"learning differences." (Teddy has a learning difference, poor boy.)

Neither the word *reading* nor the word *phonics* appears in the index.

Important Note: The federal law for the education of handicapped children says that an individual educational program (IEP) must be set up for each handicapped child. The child's parents must be invited to the meeting at which this program is decided on. They have the right to speak up and can refuse to consent to the final decision.

I would suggest to one or both parents of a learning-disabled child that they submit to the meeting the following statement:

I (We) am (are) the parent(s) of _____(name).

I (We) insist that systematic, sequential phonics ("phonics-first") should be used in teaching my (our) child to read and write, using Open Court, Lippincott, Economy, Distar, Addison-Wesley, Orton-Gillingham, Slingerland, Spalding, Traub, or any other system listed in the bibliography published by the Reading Reform Foundation, 7054 East Indian School Road, Scottsdale, Ariz. 85251.

Under no circumstances must my (our) child be taught by using the method or materials of the conventional "look-and-say" method, whether called "sight reading method," "whole-word method," "eclectic method," "combination method," or by any other name. I (We) refer particularly to the systems put out by Scott, Foresman & Co., Houghton Mifflin Co., Ginn & Co., Macmillan, Rand McNally, Laidlaw Brothers, American Book Co., Allyn & Bacon, and other so-called conventional basal commercial reader series.

I suggest that you copy this statement verbatim and file it at the meeting. I also recommend that you veto or strongly protest any other procedure or subterfuge. You can take a lawyer *and* a reading expert to the meeting. If necessary, make use of any appeals procedure your state allows.

I recommend that you take these steps whether your child is classified as "learning disabled" or as handicapped in any other way—spastic, epileptic, visually handicapped, kidney-diseased, or whatever. After all, every child receiving federal money for his education is entitled to the best education available and should be protected from the harmful effects of look-and-say.

13

"It's the Parents' Fault"

Once upon a time—around 1908 when Edmund Burke Huey wrote his famous book *The Psychology and Pedagogy of Reading*—there lived a little boy in or around Boston, Massachusetts. His parents were well-to-do, kept a staff of servants, and had plenty of leisure time on their hands. The house was large and comfortable and contained a cozy library, with a plentiful collection of favorite children's books on some lower shelves.

One day Dr. Huey came for a visit. The boy was four years old at the time.

He had never tried to read, but had a new pictured storybook which contained lines from Old Mother Hubbard. He knew the story already, but had me read it aloud over and over again, following my finger over the lines and also keeping the place by the pictures. He would then "read" by turns with me, and actually came to keep his fingers "on the place" throughout, at the first sitting. All that is needed is books of good old jingles and rhymes and folk stories and fairy tales, with illustrative pictures, and a mother or father or friend who cares enough for children to play this way and read aloud to them. The child will keep it up by the hour and the week and the month, and his natural learning to read is only a question of time.

Huey's recipe for teaching reading is almost exactly what is being followed to this day in most of our schools. They *expect* the child to be taught by this miraculous method *at home* and are sorely disappointed if the parents leave them in the lurch.

Huey's book devotes two chapters to the teaching of read-

149

ing—one, "teaching at home" by the "natural" method just
described, and another one, of equal length, on "teaching at
school." On page 334, at the end of home teaching he says
casually, "Of course there comes a time when *phonics* should
be taught . . . but that task may well be left to the school."
Later he says that phonics is dangerous before the age of nine.

To judge from the look-and-say teacher's manuals of the
1980s, it's perfectly clear that the schools still rely on home
teaching just as much as Huey did. Word-by-word-taught reading is impossible to teach in the few snatches of time the normal
modern school gives to the individual child. There has to be
enough time for one-person tutoring, and that person, by neces-
sity, is the mother rather than the schoolteacher with her full
classroom and innumerable other chores.

And so the schools assume that the parents play an enormous
part in teaching the small child to read, and they're consciously
or unconsciously fiercely resentful when parents fall down on
that unspoken contract.

A recent article by Mostafa Rejai in the *Educational Forum*
says petulantly:

> Parents have virtually abdicated their responsibility in
> helping educate their children. A tradition exists in many
> countries—as it once did in this one—where parents take
> an active and continuing part in cultivating a habit of
> reading, writing and correct speech in their children.
> They begin by helping the child through *Treasure Island,
> Alice in Wonderland,* and the like, and continue to see
> to it that the child learns to read, write and speak properly.
> Unless reading, writing and speaking are *habituated* and
> *internalized* on a round-the-clock basis, a few hours of
> school work on a five day week, nine months a year basis,
> can hardly be expected to educate the child. . . .
>
> The prevailing attitude of many parents in this country
> today is to "send Johnny to school" and then to wash
> their hands of any responsibility for his education. When
> at home, it is much easier for all parties concerned to
> have Johnny sit in front of a television set (while parents
> sit in front of another) than spending a few hours helping
> Johnny cultivate reading, writing and speaking skills.

And so the responsibility for Johnny's reading trouble is
neatly placed on his parents' shoulders. There isn't a single
piece of advice to parents from the look-and-say people that
doesn't recommend lots and lots of time reading aloud to the
child, letting him or her see the words on the page. This will
make the child memorize the words and sooner or later the
Huey-type miracle is going to happen.

There's no lack of advice on exactly how the mother is supposed to proceed. (The father is now out of it. It's assumed
that he's hard at work at the office during the day and comes
home too tired to read aloud to Johnny.)

Here's the advice of Professor James E. Flood in the May
1977 *Reading Teacher.* It was based on an elaborate experiment
with thirty-six four-year-old children in the San Francisco Bay
Area.

Each of the thirty-six children was observed at home while
his or her mother read aloud Marjorie Flack's *Ask Mr. Bear,*
a well-known children's book. Each session was tape-recorded.

Before the reading sessions, each child was asked to take
part in several "prereading tasks": alphabet recognition, whole-
word recognition, vocabulary, visual discrimination and recognition, and reproduction of geometric shapes. Their performance on those tasks was analyzed and an overall score for
each child was figured out.

After the reading sessions had been finished, the tapes were
analyzed in fourteen different ways—related remarks by the
mothers, unrelated remarks, questions by the child, warmup
questions, interruptions, after-story evaluations, and so on.

When he'd assembled all the material, Professor Flood correlated his figures. He found significant statistical correlations of
six items with good prereading scores:

1. Total number of words the child spoke.
2. Number of questions the child answered.
3. Number of questions the child asked.
4. Warmup questions asked by the mother.
5. After-story questions asked by the mother.
6. Later positive reinforcement by the mother.

From this Professor Flood deduced four pieces of advice
for parents reading aloud to their children:

1. Start the reading with some warmup questions.
2. Interrupt the reading often with questions to see whether the child is following the story.
3. Interrupt the reading often to repeat what the book says.
4. Go over the story again when you're through.

Somewhat different advice comes from Professor C. Thomas Pickering, who wrote a book, *Helping Children Learn to Read.*

> Children who are read to regularly [he writes] will become interested in certain words in stories and books. They may spontaneously learn to recognize the names of key characters (Peter Rabbit, Cinderella, Sammy the Seal, for example) and they will almost certainly learn those words if the words are called to their attention regularly (pointed out) when the stories are read. Other words may be learned by repeatedly focusing the child's attention on the word.

A third kind of advice was based on an elaborate experiment with two children in a largely middle-class school in a small semirural town in Virginia. There Professor Kenneth Hoskisson and two associates conducted an experiment in what he called "assisted reading."

They picked two children. One was Paul, aged nine, who was repeating second grade. His father was a Mexican-American construction worker; the mother was born in Germany.

The other child, Susie, was six and came from a Native American family.

Both were slow readers. Paul was wholly turned off and always refused to take part in reading class. Susie did the same. When asked why, she simply answered, "I hate reading."

The experiment lasted through the four last months of second grade. Both mothers were extremely cooperative. At a preliminary meeting they "were cautioned to let the children read at their natural pace and to give corrections only when requested." In addition, they were instructed to avoid any criticism of the children while they were reading. They were asked to read with the child at a pleasant time of the day when other activities, such as playing outside or a favorite TV show, would not conflict with the reading time. Reading time was restricted to from three to five fifteen- to twenty-minute sessions per week.

The parents were informed verbally of several ways in which they could reinforce their children for reading and when to deliver this reinforcement. Examples of possible reinforcers were saying "that's correct," exclaiming "good" or "right" and physical contact. The parents were asked to give all such reinforcers immediately after a correct response, particularly after self-initiated responses. In addition, it was suggested that, at least initially, special privileges such as a favorite drink or candy be made available, following the reading session.

In addition to those sessions with their mothers, Paul and Susie also were exposed to a "listening post" in class, where they could listen to recorded reading while they were looking at the corresponding pages in their readers. (The class used the Ginn 360 look-and-say series.) Then there was also "peer tutoring" once a week, when Paul and Susie read with a "reading partner" who overheard their reading.

The result of all these efforts was meager. Paul, who had repeated the second grade, went up to the middle of third-grade level after the four months; Susie rose from a first-grade to a second-grade score, but gained almost nothing in vocabulary.

Undeterred, Professor Hoskisson and his associates celebrated this outcome as a great victory. They were particularly proud that the mothers "quickly learned to reinforce their children for correct responses and to supply unknown words to the children in a non-threatening manner."

So there you have it. The "official" way to check on your children's reading progress is to supply all the words they don't know, saying "that's right" after all the words they do know, and give them candy or a soft drink each time they're through with their reading.

Professor Hoskisson doesn't say, but presumably what the children read to their mothers was the stories they'd learned in school from their Ginn readers and had rehearsed again and again with the tape recorder and the "peer tutor."

After all, those were the only stories they'd learned to read. And, even so, if they didn't know a specific word, Mother was told to tell them the word in "a non-threatening manner." All this and candy too—the perfect example of look-and-say in all its glory.

And now, after these edifying examples of what our educators expect from their pupils' parents, let me tell you an interesting story from Israel.

Back in 1952, the Israeli scholar Jacob Levy published an influential article, in which he recommended the American-type look-and-say system for teaching beginning readers the Hebrew language. This was quickly introduced in many schools. However, after the mass immigration of Jews from Syria, Morocco, and other Arab countries in the early fifties it was soon found that Levy's system didn't work. Mass failure rates of 50 percent or more pupils became common.

A study of ten first-grade classes brought the astonishing result that nine of them did very poorly, but one of them did well.

It didn't take long to solve the puzzle. The nine poorly performing classes were full of children from poor, Mideast-immigrant homes, while the one exceptional class consisted of the children of Jews who'd come from Europe.

Why? Because the children had taken their classwork and showed it to their parents. The Mideast-immigrant parents, often themselves illiterate, hadn't taken any particular interest, but the European fathers and mothers were appalled. They exploded in anger and in short order taught their children the Hebrew alphabet and how it was applied in writing. "We thought our son read very well and were delighted with his progress," one father said. "But when he fell ill in the middle of the term we suddenly discovered that all he did was guess. So I explained the principle of the thing to him and by the time he returned to school a few days later he could really read."

A mother echoed this: "With my first daughter I still believed the parents should not interfere. Poor her, she still had difficulties in the third grade. With the other two I didn't wait. I taught them right from the beginning. They had no problems and read well before the end of the year!"

The Israeli Ministry of Education drew the only possible conclusion from this. They reinstated phonics-first in all schools. A 1966 survey showed that *all* Israeli first-graders read better than ever.

All I can say to American parents is, Follow the example of those enlightened Israeli fathers and mothers. Foil the system. Stamp out the disease before your child gets infected. Teach your child by phonics at home before he enters a school that follows the look-and-say method.

You don't have to do this very systematically. Just do more or less the opposite of what is recommended by the look-and-say educators. By all means, read to your child and let him or her see the pages you're reading from. But instead of focusing on the words and their meanings, draw their attention to the letters.

Show them how the letters are pronounced. Sound out easy words for them and let them do it after you. Tell them and remind them often that letters correspond to sounds.

Buy them alphabet blocks. Put letters or letter charts on the wall. Get them a simple ABC book. Play school. Let them "solve" such simple words as *fig* or *pet*.

If they show any inclination to invented spelling like KUM AND HAV FUN, let them go ahead. They'll learn the correct spelling soon enough when they go to school.

You can start all this when they're four or so. As I said, Montessori thought this was the best age. If you can, get or make them some educational tools like sandpaper letters and such. Read letters aloud to them and let them look at anything written or printed that's around. Answer all their questions about writing. Let them scribble to their hearts' content. Yours should be a home with an infinity of paper, pencils, and crayons. Maybe get a little blackboard also. See to it that they're surrounded by letters.

Play letter and rhyming games with them. If there is an older brother and sister, use the opportunity and let the older teach the younger.

If you do all that, there'll be a moment sooner or later when the child catches on to the alphabetic principle. Once this happens, you've won. It'll be only weeks before he or she starts reading and writing.

If you notice signs of a special-interest "binge," exploit it. It may be cooking or coins or miniature cars. Whatever it is, hook it up to letters and writing somehow. Same with TV. Don't shut off the TV, put it to work as an educator. I'll tell you more about that in the next chapter.

If you're ambitious and want to do a real job of it, get an instruction book and do the thing systematically. My own book, *Why Johnny Can't Read—And What You Can Do About It* is available everywhere in an inexpensive paperback edition. Many thousands have used its 72 exercises and taught their children in a short time. If you can't get it locally, write to Harper & Row, 10 East 53rd Street, New York, N.Y. 10022. You can order it by mail.

Of course, there are plenty of other phonic texts available. Write to the Reading Reform Foundation, 7054 East Indian School Road, Scottsdale, Arizona 85251, for a list.

In other words, beat the system. There's no special knowledge necessary, as long as you can read and write yourself and can follow easy directions. Send your child to kindergarten or first grade immune to reading trouble and you'll have done wonders for his or her education.

14

"Too Much TV"

Little John was *not* a child prodigy.

On the contrary, little John was just an average black child, growing up in a Southern large city as one of five children of a lower-middle-class black family—with one exception: At the age of four it was discovered that John could read. Not just a few letters, but virtually anything he was given to read. If he didn't know a word, he skipped it, but otherwise he read fluently, with perfect intonation, obviously taking in the meaning of what he was reading.

Dr. Jane W. Torrey, a psychology professor at Connecticut College in New London, took the opportunity to spend three hours a week for four months with him and made notes of her observations. She published them in 1969 in the journal *Elementary English.*

She found that nobody had taught John anything. His mother was totally surprised when she heard him read from a cereal box, and so were other family members, particularly his grandmother. They questioned John about his reading and he insisted he'd learned it all by himself from TV commercials. He'd started by figuring out words like *Ban* and *Sominex,* which had appeared on the screen with the announcer pronouncing them at the same time, and he'd gone on from there, gradually figuring out the phonetic system of English writing.

He had an older brother and an older sister, both of whom were taught to read in school. But he was way ahead of them and occasionally helped *them* with their reading.

John's father was a truck driver and his mother worked as a maid in a hospital. The father had had about eight years of schooling and the mother about ten. With five children, they had a combined income that was low enough to entitle them to a housing subsidy, but did not put them into the poverty bracket.

John's mother said simply that his reading was a gift from God. But she told Dr. Torrey that at the age of four he'd always listened avidly to TV commercials and was able to recite them from memory. He was fascinated by them and never paid any attention to anything else while they were shown. Dr. Torrey checked and found that an average of forty words per hour are normally shown and pronounced at the same time. On children's programs many of those words are also shown on labels and boxes. His grandmother discovered that John could read when he started to read the brand names off the cans and boxes.

John's IQ of 104 was average, like that of most children in the Durkin study I mentioned in Chapter 11. His interest in reading was quite spontaneous and started with a general interest in letters and numbers, which he tried to satisfy as best he could. The TV commercials were the best available source.

He was particularly fond of his eleven-year-old brother and sometimes read stories to him from books. The brother himself couldn't do this alone.

Dr. Torrey tried her best to find out who had taught him to read but couldn't find any other source of his knowledge. She cross-examined John's mother, but the mother steadfastly refused to say she'd helped him. It was all a complete surprise to her and to John's grandmother. At first she'd been afraid he'd damage the library books his sister brought home, but then one day she found him reading aloud to guests out of a third-grade reader.

Dr. Torrey was left with the TV commercials as the only known source of John's reading ability.

> Commercials [she wrote] are frequently repeated, so that whatever a child fails to learn in one showing can be drilled ad nauseam in subsequent days and weeks. Commercials are designed to get attention, so they are usually loud, lively and simple. Memorizing of short sentences is facilitated by catchy tunes. Many common words are shown and the unfamiliar brand names (e.g., "Ban," "Sominex") are usually short or easy to pronounce. It

seems possible that from commercials a child could get a start on a basic vocabulary and make a few inferences about phonics, extend his reading knowledge through phonics, use the redundancy of language in simple books, ask occasional questions and be corrected by an adult.

Dr. Torrey described John's way of reading in great detail. The most astonishing fact was that he normally spoke typical black dialect English, but read standard English without trouble. Also, whenever he dictated to her, he made an effort to speak standard English.

His spelling was excellent, even though it sometimes differed from his pronunciation. For instance, John once said in conversation, "They were tired of shopping over there. Buying toys for Christmas for the ch???s."
Dr. Torrey said, "Toys for the what?"
John: "Ch???s."
Dr. Torrey: "Oh, churches."
John: "Uh-uh, ch???s."
Dr. Torrey: "Turkeys?"
John: "Uh-uh, chrns." (Louder and very carefully articulated.)
Dr. Torrey: "Can you spell it?"
John: "C.H.I.L.D.R.E.N."
Although he'd three times pronounced the final *s* of his own dialect, he spelled the word correctly without the final *s* when he was asked to.

At another occasion he was asked to read the following two lines:

> The bunny now gets twenty hops,
> While in the woods the lolly pops.

He read the little verse without hesitation, giving the word "pops" the right verb intonation the sentence called for.
Another verse he read was this:

> Two more hops for the bunny and then
> Look out for the Pipsissewah in his den.

He had no trouble at all with the word "Pipsissewah."
Once Dr. Torrey gave him a French picture dictionary to read. He cheerfully read the words one after another, pronouncing them as if they were English words. The fact that

he didn't understand what he was reading didn't seem to bother him.

Whenever Dr. Torrey asked him to read a lengthy passage aloud to her, he refused. He said she could read it herself.

He could also write, although he was a little better with capitals than with lower-case letters. He'd write little messages to Dr. Torrey: "Put candy in the machine." "Look under the table." Once, tongue in cheek, he wrote, "Jump rope." Another time he wrote simply, "Get out."

As I said, John's IQ of 104 was about average. "There is no evidence," Dr. Torrey wrote, "that his extraordinary reading ability is a matter of unusually high intelligence, or of extraordinary verbal ability."

After two months in the first grade John's reading was tested routinely. His reading ability was 4.8 (eighth month of the fourth grade) and his spelling was at 5.0 (start of fifth grade.)

Dr. Torrey concluded:

> However useful high verbal ability and high cultural privilege may be in stimulating reading, neither is necessary.
>
> John has no more than average tested verbal ability and perhaps even less than average cultural stimulation in the direction of reading. The key factor in reading therefore must be something else. Large vocabulary, sophisticated thinking, accurate articulation of standard English, active encouragement and instruction in reading skills, may very well help a child learn to read. However, even a single case like John's shows they are not indispensable, that is, that neither success nor failure in reading can be predicted in individual cases from these factors alone.

To me, these findings and conclusions prove clearly that much of what is written about how to raise reading "readiness" or ability is quite wrong. The philosopher William James said that the proven existence of one white crow proves conclusively that not all crows are black. In the same way, the existence of little John proves that "disadvantaged," "culturally deprived" non-standard-English-speaking children can learn to read just as well as those from more affluent homes.

And what else does Dr. Torrey's study prove? It proves that TV, *particularly commercials,* is an excellent tool for learning how to read. The steady repetition, so nauseating to the average middle-class adult, makes a splendid, inexorable drill for the student. The use of the voice-over spoken message synchronized with the printed words on the screen seems to be the key. It's the ideal way to show a child that our way of writing is based on the matching of spelling and sound.

Please note that among the 205 early readers observed by Dr. Dolores Durkin, a large number learned from TV commercials. Two of them, Jack and Mark, are mentioned in my Chapter 11. TV, far from being an obstacle to reading instruction, is, at the beginner's level, a profound blessing.

Of course, that's exactly contrary to the popular cliché. During the writing of this book, I've talked to many of my friends and acquaintances about the reading problem. Invariably the first reaction is an accusation of TV. "They don't read any good books any more because they spend all their time watching TV" is the standard view. In truth, it's just the other way around. The kids haven't been taught to read fluently and so they use their leisure hours to watch TV. Reading for them is a painful chore. How can anyone expect them to turn to leisure reading voluntarily? They're astronomically far away from the stage of reading a book because it's *enjoyable.*

On the other hand, consider the enormous advantages of TV for a child's mind and intellectual progress. By now virtually every American home, no matter how poor, has a TV set. Consider what this does to the mental horizon of a small child. The change that has come to this country is fantastic. Our children know vastly more things than we used to know at their age. Their vocabulary, which was once estimated at 24,000 words at age six, is by now probably 30,000 or more. Their sophistication in many other ways is astounding.

In the fall of 1977 Dr. Robert L. Thorndike of Teachers College, Columbia University, wrote an article in the *Journal of Educational Measurement,* in which he explained why the standard Stanford-Binet IQ test was restandardized in 1972. Among the factors he mentioned that accounted for the ten-point lowering of the measure—that is, increase of the observed general intelligence—TV was one of the most prominent.

"TV," he told me, "is good for children up to about grade four. After that, the situation is reversed."

Yes, from the point of view of teaching children to read, TV is a great blessing—a national treasure.

In addition, there has been an impact from the two TV shows that have been shown to children over public television—*Sesame Street* and *The Electric Company*. Again, Dr. Thorndike was sure that these two shows had had a considerable influence in raising small children's IQ, but it was impossible for him to estimate how much. There had been too many uncertain factors—the fact that public television didn't reach all homes, the fact that *Sesame Street* was mainly aimed at preschool children, while *The Electric Company* was designed for second-graders lagging in reading, and many others. So all we know is that the small children of today are smarter than those of fifty years ago, but there's no way of telling exactly why this is so.

There is no doubt that millions of children have profited from watching *Sesame Street* and through it have become familiar with letters and figures. There's also no doubt that *The Electric Company* has helped many kids who had been having reading trouble in school. But in the summer of 1975 the slant of that program was shifted away from straightforward phonics, so that now it is far less intensive in its teaching than it used to be. In 1977, after two more years, production of *The Electric Company* stopped altogether and only reruns are now being shown—of the last two seasons only.

So the two public service programs didn't turn out to be as revolutionary a breakthrough as they were meant to be. Still, TV has enormous potential for teaching beginners to read. I'm still waiting for the enlightened top executive of one of the big TV advertisers who'll emphasize simultaneous voice-overs of simple words, shown in big letters on the screen. He'll cause thousands, maybe millions of Montessori-type individual "reading explosions."

And, once a child has fully understood the connection between sounds and letters, there's no stopping him from becoming a fluent reader almost overnight.

Like little John.

15

"We Now Teach *All* Children"

In 1969, Professor Arthur R. Jensen wrote a much-discussed racist article for the *Harvard Educational Review*. It began with the words, "Compensatory education has been tried and it apparently has failed."

Nine years later, in 1978, the same *Harvard Educational Review* carried an article in which three U.S. Office of Education staff members wrote: "Compensatory education can work. There were enough instances of success in enough sites to suggest that the Follow Through children did better than they would have done in the absence of the program, indicating that special efforts on behalf of disadvantaged children can indeed yield results." The sentence referred to the Distar phonic system of teaching reading.

Professor Jensen's racist article belongs now to history, bearing the burden of being based mainly on data by the late English psychologist Cyril M. Burt, which were long ago revealed as having been faked. The newer studies prove that *compensatory education works if reading is taught by phonics.*

In the November 1977 issue of *Reading Teacher,* Dr. John Guthrie described the Distar program in more detail: "Project Follow Through," he wrote, "was planned as a large-scale teaching program for disadvantaged children during the Johnson Administration of 1967, but was transformed into a series of 'planned variations of education.'" By far the best performing of those variations was Distar, developed at the University of Oregon, "consistently falling into the top of the group."

"The Direct Instruction model (Distar)," Dr. Guthrie wrote, "aims to increase learning of disadvantaged children in reading, language and arithmetic. Through tightly structured material

163

and careful teacher training, children are taught specific skills that follow a task analysis. . . . The teaching program that is used can be seen to make a consistent difference in achievement."

Despite the spectacular success of Distar in the Follow Through series, most American educators remained pessimistic. For instance, in *The Reading Teacher* for January 1977, Professor Orvel A. Criqui, principal of the South Junior High School in Lawrence, Kansas, wrote:

> Evidence appears to indicate that every child with normal intelligence can *not* be brought up to grade level. . . .
>
> We should explain that all students can *not* be taught to read at grade level or above. There are many reasons why this desirable goal cannot be reached. According to recent research, reading disabilities are persistent. Excellent teaching will usually not help the poor reader to "catch up." It seems that with special tutoring the poor reader may show a brief period of accelerated growth, but the poor reader who has been making a half year's progress in reading each year, after the period of acceleration, will probably continue at the original rate of growth.
>
> Although it is desirable for all students to read at or above grade level, it must be remembered that the tests are designed so that this cannot reasonably be expected. A staff member who understands test construction and interpretation and can explain testing in explicit terms should give the information to the community.

This common fatalistic attitude was described in detail by Dr. Mary Rhodes Hoover in the April 1978 issue of *The Reading Teacher*. Dr. Hoover had attended about a hundred teachers' workshops around the country and compiled the following list of "blame the victim" statements:

Minority students can't learn to read because:

—their IQs are low, showing minimal cognitive skills.
—their language is so broken as to be no language at all.
—they have a language but it's so restricted that it hinders them in learning.

—they can't think abstractly so we can teach them only what they concretely memorize; we must, therefore, stay away from phonics or higher level mathematics for these children.

—they can't hear. Their homes are so noisy that their auditory discrimination, so necessary for reading, is impaired.

—they're culturally deprived.

—the parents don't care.

—they're poor. None of the poor can read. In fact, none of the world's poor can read.

—they're emotionally disturbed. Their homes are battlegrounds. We must love them, and make them whole again.

—they can't read Standard English. Their language interferes, having different sound-symbol correspondences. We are thus restricted to the use of the language experience approach in teaching.

—Standard English texts are too "nice" (non-profane). They need to read spicier things.

—they are not motivated and so they forget how to read.

—they're passive and need to be taught how to control their lives.

—they're violent and need counseling and not teaching.

—they're culturally different and their culture doesn't value reading. Their peers don't value it; their parents don't value it.

—their self-concepts are too low. We must first improve the self-concept and *then* they can learn to read.

—they're not sitting next to whites. Black children must be exposed to whites before they will be motivated to learn to read.

—they're being rushed. We must wait until they're ready—even if we wait until adolescence before we teach reading.

—they know that if we teach them to read they will be brainwashed by ruling class propaganda.

—they have an oral tradition. We can't expect them to adapt to written material.

—their family structure is different and not responsive to homework needs, etc.

After this devastating list of alibis, Dr. Hoover listed fifteen black schools that had shown excellent results in teaching black children to read. Each of the fifteen used a phonics-first system.

I could add hundreds of other such schools to her list. Each of the phonics publishers I got in touch with sent me a stack of statistical studies showing that phonics worked better than look-and-say. *It worked better with children of all races and backgrounds, the physically handicapped, the emotionally disturbed and the severely mentally retarded.*

At this point, this is no longer surprising, since a long, long series of studies has shown that carefully structured, sequential phonics is astronomically better than the disorderly mishmash look-and-say teacher's manuals are usually filled with.

Recently I read about a particularly telling example of the difference between the two systems. Miss Ann M. Doyle, a reporter for the West Palm Beach, Florida, *Post,* wrote the story of the school in Grand Ridge, Florida.

Grand Ridge is a small town in the Florida panhandle with a population of 540 people. Until 1974 its school had used one of the Dismal Dozen reading systems, with the usual unhappy results. Average reading achievement was about one grade behind the national norm. The teachers were unhappy, the parents were unhappy, and the principal, Mr. Joseph Houston, was unhappy. So they looked around for a better system. It turned out that 30 percent of Florida's private schools used the Open Court system and the school board members liked what they saw on their inspections and visits. The board decided to adopt Open Court.

Then it turned out there was not enough money in that year's budget to buy the new series. But the parents were undeterred. They started spaghetti and chicken suppers, strawberry festivals, Halloween parties, door-to-door soliciting, and whatever else they could think of. They even raffled off a cow, which brought in a tidy $900. Administrators sold Tupperware. Teachers sold Grand Ridge T-shirts.

At last all the money was raised and the next first grade started with Open Court.

By the end of the first semester results began to come in: "The children proved us right," one mother said. "I have a little girl that started with Open Court. . . . She didn't have any special help at home. Her reading ability is outstanding."

And a teacher said, "If you rate a Cadillac and a Toyota, we have the Cadillac. In all my years it does the job I've wanted to be done."

That just about sums up what happens in a school when you switch from look-and-say to phonics-first.

In the spring of 1980, about a year after my visit to P.S. 251 in Brooklyn, I visited P.S. 30 in Jamaica, Queens, New York City. Guided by the principal, Mrs. Ursula Day, I visited and observed many first- and second-grade classes.

The results of using the Lippincott system were just about the same as I'd seen in P.S. 251, where Open Court is being used. The same eager faces, the same forest of raised hands in answer to questions, the same proficiency in reading after a semester or a year.

One second-grade black boy named Roger—the school is all-black—read to me aloud from a monster book he'd never seen: "But before the mailman came, a stamp-collecting Trollusk crept up to the mailbox, stole the letter and gabbled away with a smirk on his snerk."

I asked Roger whether he knew what *smirk* meant.

"Grin," he said, grinning.

To make sure once more, I also visited the schools in Mount Vernon, New York, which had adopted the Distar system. I found everybody happy, children reading with vim and vigor, and nothing but enthusiasm for phonics-first. (The schools are 75 percent black.)

Finally I visited the Fortune Society in New York City, where a group of incredibly patient volunteers help illiterate ex-offenders to new, productive lives. The job usually takes about a year—using a phonics-first system, of course—and gives new hope to seemingly hopeless victims of look-and-say.

But why, you may well ask, don't we have phonics-first in all our schools and kick out look-and-say once and for all?

You may well ask. I cannot answer the question, but I can introduce the most unimpeachable witness of them all, Professor William K. Durr, senior author of the Houghton Mifflin look-and-say series, the leading publisher of conventional readers.

In November 1974 Professor Durr reported on a study trip

to Russia in the pages of *The Reading Teacher*. He'd spent ten days in intense discussion with Russian educational leaders and visited classrooms in Moscow, Leningrad, and Tashkent.

He found that first-graders are taught to read 46 of the 130 national languages of Russia. They start at age seven in first grade, but most of them have been in day care centers in the years before and learned to read in those centers. In Moscow about 50 percent of the children come to school already able to read.

All children in the USSR are given an ABC book and start to learn from it the day school begins. They learn at first about a letter a day and what it stands for, and gradually proceed to syllables and words.

By December 15 of their first year all Russian children are through with their ABC books and start reading simple stories and poems. There is no further instruction in reading as such after the end of first grade.

> When children enter grade one [Professor Durr wrote], there is an expectation that they will learn to read and that they will progress evenly through the reading sequence. At the end of grade one, it is found that approximately 2 to 3 percent of the pupils have not attained the required level of reading proficiency. These pupils are referred to a medical commission for diagnosis. Of the total school population, about 1 percent are diagnosed as mentally retarded and placed in special classes. The remaining one or two out of 100 who have not passed the end of the grade examination repeat the same grade again. Since no medical reason has been found for failure, it is expected that the teacher will insure the child's success the second time through grade one. . . .
>
> *Two correlates of reading difficulties which are sometimes cited in the United States are perceptual problems and low socioeconomic background. Soviet authorities completely dismiss both of these as bases for reading deficiencies. They contend their research disproves any relationship between either of these factors and reading achievement. . . .*
>
> *It appears that Soviet children do learn to read effec-*

tively at an early age. If this conclusion is correct, the obvious question is "Why?"

Professor Durr doesn't really answer this question. He winds up:

> The common dedication to the goal of literacy coupled with the conviction that this goal can and will be attained seems to be of greater significance to the young Soviet child as he achieves success in reading.

But the true explanation appears in an earlier observation by Professor Durr: "The emphasis in the Soviet Union is on learning individual letter-sound associations. *No words are taught by the sight method.*"

References

Chapter 1: Why Johnny *Still* Can't Read

Page
1   Flesch, Rudolf. *Why Johnny Can't Read—And What You
     Can Do About It*. New York, Harper & Row, 1955.

1   *Final Report on the Adult Performance Level Study*. Univer-
     sity of Texas at Austin, 1975.

2   Maeroff, Gene L. "Scores on Scholastic Aptitude Tests Con-
     tinue to Drop." *New York Times*, October 5, 1980, p.
     29.

2   *On Further Examination*. College Entrance Examination
     Board. New York, 1977.

2   Chall, Jeanne S.; Conrad, S. S.; and Harris, S. H. *An Analysis
     of Textbooks in Relation to Declining SAT Scores*. Col-
     lege Entrance Examination Board. New York, 1977,
     p. 62.

Chapter 2: History of a Gimmick

Page
15   Mathews, Mitford M. *Teaching to Read, Historically Con-
     sidered*. University of Chicago Press, 1966.

19   Farnham, George L. *The Sentence Method of Teaching
     Reading, Writing, and Spelling*. (2nd ed.) Syracuse,
     N.Y., 1887.

20   Parker, Francis W. *Talks on Pedagogics*. New York, A. S.
     Barnes, 1894.

21   Harrison, Gilbert A. *A Timeless Affair: The Life of Anita
     McCormick Blaine*. University of Chicago Press, 1979.

21   Huey, Edmund Burke. *The Psychology and Pedagogy of
     Reading*. New York, Macmillan, 1908.

24   Goodman, Kenneth. "Reading: A Psycholinguistic Guessing
     Game." In Singer, Harry, and Ruddell, Robert B., eds.,
     Theoretical Models and Processes of Reading. (2nd ed.)
     Newark, Del., International Reading Association, 1976,
     pp. 497–508.

Page
24   Spiegel, Dixie L. "Meaning-Seeking Strategies for the Begin-
        ning Reader." *Reading Teacher,* April 1978, pp. 772–
        776.
25   Sherman, Barry. "Reading for Meaning." *Learning,* Novem-
        ber 1979, pp. 41–44.
26   Fiske, Edward B. "Approach to Reading Rethought" (inter-
        view with Kenneth Goodman). *New York Times,* July
        9, 1973.
26   Smith, Frank. *Understanding Reading.* New York, Holt,
        Rinehart & Winston, 1971.
26   ——. *Psycholinguistics and Reading.* New York, Holt, Rine-
        hart & Winston, 1973.
26   ——. *Reading Without Nonsense.* New York, Teachers Col-
        lege Press, 1979.

Chapter 3: Look-and-Say Exposed

Page
28   Mathews, *Teaching to Read* (see Chapter 2), p. 148.
29   Gurren, Louise, and Hughes, Ann. "Intensive Phonics vs.
        Gradual Phonics in Beginning Reading: A Review."
        Journal of Educational Research, vol. 58, no. 8, April
        1965, pp. 339–346.
29   Chall, Jeanne S. *Learning to Read: The Great Debate.* New
        York, McGraw-Hill, 1967.
30   Walcutt, Charles C.; Lamport, J.; and McCracken, G. *Teach-
        ing Reading.* New York, Macmillan, 1974. (Chapters
        on research and evaluation by Robert Dykstra.)
31   Kelly, Barbara C. "The Economy Method versus the Scott
        Foresman Method in Teaching Second-Grade Reading
        in the Murphysboro Public Schools." *Journal of Educa-
        tional Research,* vol. 50, February 1958, pp. 465–
        468.
32   Becker, Wesley C., and Engelmann, Siegfried. *Analysis of
        Achievement Data on Six Cohorts of Low-Income Chil-
        dren from 20 School Districts in the University of Ore-
        gon Direct Instruction Follow Through Model
        (Technical Report 78—1).* University of Oregon College
        of Education Follow Through Project, Eugene, Ore.,
        December 1978.
32   Cattell, James McKeen. "The Time It Takes to See and
        Name Objects." *Mind,* vol. 11, 1886, pp. 63–65.

Page

33   Marchbanks, Gabrielle, and Levin, Harry. "Cues by Which Children Recognize Words." *Journal of Educational Psychology*, 1965, vol. 56, no. 2, pp. 57–61.

33   Timko, Henry G. "Configuration as a Cue in the Word Recognition of Beginning Readers." *Journal of Experimental Education*, vol. 39, 1970, pp. 68–69.

33   Williams, Joanna P.; Blumberg, E. L.; and Williams, D. V. "Cues Used in Visual Word Recognition." *Journal of Educational Psychology*, vol. 61, 1970, pp. 310–315.

33   Bishop, Carol H. "Transfer Effects of Word and Letter Training in Reading." *Journal of Verbal Learning & Verbal Behavior*, vol. 3, 1964, pp. 215–221.

34   Jeffrey, W. E., and Samuels, S. J. "Effect of Method of Reading Training on Initial Learning and Transfer." *Journal of Verbal Learning & Verbal Behavior*, vol. 6, 1967, pp. 354–358.

34   Carnine, Douglas W. "Phonics vs. Look-Say: Transfer to New Words." *Reading Teacher*, March 1977, pp. 636–640.

35   Gagné, Robert M. "The Acquisition of Knowledge." *Psychological Review*, 1962, vol. 69, no. 4, pp. 355–365.

35   ———. *The Conditions of Learning.* New York, Holt, Rinehart & Winston, 1965.

36   Samuels, S. Jay. "Hierarchical Subskills in the Reading Acquisition Process." In Guthrie, J., ed. *Aspects of Reading Acquisition.* Baltimore, Johns Hopkins University Press, 1976, pp. 162–179.

37   Resnick, Lauren B., and Weaver, P. A., eds. *Theory and Practice of Early Reading.* Hillsdale, N.J., Lawrence Erlbaum Associates, 1979. 3 vols.

37   Williams, Joanna. "The ABD's of Reading: A Program for the Learning Disabled." In Resnick and Weaver, eds., *Theory and Practice . . .* (see above), vol. 3.

37   Weaver, Phyllis A., and Resnick, L. B. "The Theory and Practice of Early Reading: An Introduction." In Resnick and Weaver, eds. *Theory and Practice . . .* (see above), vol. 1.

38   Resnick, Lauren B. "Theories and Prescriptions for Early Reading Instruction." In Resnick & Weaver, eds. *Theory and Practice . . .* (see above) vol. 2, p. 329.

38   Liberman, Isabelle Y., and Shankweiler, D. "Speech, the Alphabet, and Teaching to Read." In Resnick and

Page

         Weaver, eds. *Theory and Practice* . . . (see above), vol. 2, pp. 121–122.

38   Samuels, S. Jay. "How the Mind Works When Reading: Describing Elephants No One Has Ever Seen." In Resnick and Weaver, eds. *Theory and Practice* . . . (see above), vol. 1, p. 348.

39   Bateman, Barbara. "Teaching Reading to Learning Disabled and Other Hard-to-Teach Children." In Resnick and Weaver, eds. *Theory and Practice* . . . (see above), vol. 1, p. 247.

Chapter 4: The Great Coverup

Page

40   Gates, Arthur I. *Methods in Primary Reading*. New York, Teachers College, 1928.

41   Flesch, *Why Johnny Can't Read* (see Chapter 1).

41   Chall, *Learning to Read* (see Chapter 3), p. 112.

41   "Phonics in Reading Instruction." *Reading Teacher,* December 1955.

41   Lamkin, F. Duane. "An Analysis of Propaganda Techniques Used in *Why Johnny Can't Read*—Flesch." *Reading Teacher* (see above), pp. 107–118.

41   Gray, William S. "Phonic versus Other Methods of Teaching Reading." *Reading Teacher* (see above), pp. 102–106.

41   Buswell, Guy T. *Fundamental Reading Habits: A Study of Their Development.* Supplementary Educational Monographs, no. 21. University of Chicago Press, 1922.

41   Gray, William S. *Studies of Elementary School Reading Through Standardized Tests.* Supplementary Educational Monographs, no. 1. University of Chicago Press, 1917, pp. 127–128.

42   Gurren and Hughes, "Intensive Phonics . . ." (see Chapter 3).

42   Spache, George D. and Evelyn B. *Reading in the Elementary School* (4th ed.). Boston, Allyn and Bacon, 1977.

42   Harris, Larry A., and Smith, Carl B. *Reading Instruction: Diagnostic Teaching in the Classroom* (2d ed.). New York, Holt, Rinehart & Winston, 1976.

43   Hittleman, Daniel R. *Developmental Reading: A Psycholinguistic Perspective.* Chicago, Rand McNally, 1978.

Page

43   Chall, Jeanne S. *Reading 1967–1977: A Decade of Change and Promise*. Phi Delta Kappa Fastbacks, 1977, no. 97, pp. 5–38.

43   Popp, Helen M. "Current Practices in the Teaching of Beginning Reading." In Carroll, John B., and Chall, J. S. (eds.), *Toward a Literate Society*. New York, McGraw-Hill, 1975, pp. 101–146.

44   Durr, William K. Letter to the editor of *Family Circle*, November 5, 1979.

44   Walcutt *et al. Teaching Reading* (see Chapter 3). Chapters by Dykstra.

45   Stauffer, Russell. "Some Tidy Generalization" (editorial). *Reading Teacher*, October 1966, p. 4.

45   Dykstra, Robert. "What the 27 Studies Said." *Reading Informer*, November 1977, pp. 11–12, 24.

46   House, Ernest R.; Glass, Gene V.; McLean, Leslie D.; and Walker, Decker F. "No Simple Answer: Critique of the Follow Through Evaluation." *Harvard Educational Review*, vol. 48, no. 2, 1978, pp. 128–160.

46   Wisler, Carl E.; Burns, Gerald P., Jr.; and Imamoto, David. "Follow Through Redux: A Response to the 'Critique by House, Glass, McLean and Walker." *Harvard Educational Review*, vol. 48, no. 2, 1978, pp. 171–185.

47   Samuels, S. Jay. "Effects of Pictures on Learning to Read, Comprehension and Attitudes." *Review of Educational Research*, vol. 40, no. 1, 1967, pp. 397–407.

Chapter 5: The Ten Alibis

Page

48   Flesch, Rudolf. "Why Johnny *Still* Can't Read." *Family Circle*, November 1, 1979.

57   International Reading Association. "Position Statement. 'There's More to Reading than Some Folks Say.' " *Reading Teacher*, May 1980, p. 901.

Chapter 6: "Everything Is Hunky-Dory"

Page

59   Howe, Harold II. Testimony before Senate Subcommittee on Education, Arts and Humanities, February 13, 1979.

Page

59   *Final Report on the APL Study* (see Chapter 1).

59   *Adult APL Survey* (American College Testing Program). University of Texas at Austin, 1976.

59   Hunter, Carmen St. John, and Harman, David. *Adult Illiteracy in the United States. A Report to the Ford Foundation.* New York, McGraw-Hill, 1979.

60   Farr, Roger. "Is Johnny's/Mary's Reading Getting Worse?" *Educational Leadership,* April 1977, pp. 521–527.

61   National Assessment of Educational Progress. *Reading in America: A Perspective on Two Assessments* (Reading Report No. 06-R-01). Denver, Colo., October 1976.

61   Venezky, Richard L. "NAEP—the Messenger Who Brings Bad News?" *Reading Teacher,* April 1977, pp. 750–755.

62   Chambers, Marcia. "High School Dropout Rate at 45%, Macchiarola Reports to City Board." *New York Times,* October 17, 1979, pp. A1, A12.

63   Kline, Carl L. "The Adolescents with Learning Problems: How Long Must They Wait?" *Journal of Learning Disabilities,* vol. 5, no. 5, May 1972, pp. 14–36.

64   Gindin, R. Arthur. "Spelling Performance of Medical Students." *Bulletin of the New York Academy of Medicine,* vol. 50, no. 10, November 1974, pp. 1120–1121.

64   *On Further Examination* (see Chapter 1).

68   Bishop, Margaret. "Case History of a Reluctant Reader" (unpublished article).

Chapter 7: "We Do Teach Phonics"

Page

72   Artley, A. Sterl. "Phonics Revisited." *Language Arts,* vol. 54, no. 2, February 1977, pp. 121–126.

73   Dallmann, Martha, *et al. The Teaching of Reading,* 5th ed. New York, Holt, Rinehart & Winston, 1978.

73   Heilman, Arthur. *Principles and Practices of Teaching Reading.* (4th ed.) Columbus, Ohio, Charles E. Merrill, 1977.

74   Clymer, Theodore. "The Utility of Phonic Generalizations in the Primary Grades." *Reading Teacher,* January 1963, pp. 252–257.

75   Fry, Edward. "A Frequency Approach to Phonics." *Elementary English,* vol. 6, 1964, pp. 759–765.

Page
75   Bailey, Mildred H. "An Analytical Study of the Utility of Selected Phonic Generalizations for Children in Grades One Through Six." Unpublished doctoral dissertation, Oxford, Miss., University of Mississippi, 1965.

75   Emans, R. "The Usefulness of Phonic Generalizations Above the Primary Grades." Paper given at the American Educational Research Association, Chicago, 1966.

75   Burmeister, Lou E. "Usefulness of Phonic Generalizations." *Reading Teacher*, vol. 21, no. 4, January 1968, pp. 349–356.

81   Durkin, Dolores. *Strategies for Identifying Words*. Boston, Allyn and Bacon, 1976.

82   Gough, Philip B.; Alford, J. A. Jr.; and Holley-Wilcox, P. "Words and Contexts." In Tzeng, O. J. L., and Singer, H. (eds.), *Perception of Print: Reading Research in Experimental Psychology*. Hillsdale, N.J.: Lawrence Erlbaum Associates, in press.

82   Middleton, Thomas H. "The March to Gibberish." *Saturday Review*, April 12, 1980, p. 12.

Chapter 8: "No One Method Is Best"

Page
84   Wepman, Joseph M. "Auditory Discrimination, Speech, and Reading." *Elementary School Journal*, March 1960, pp. 325–333.

84   ——. "The Perceptual Basis for Learning." In *Meeting Individual Differences in Reading*. Robinson, H. Alan, ed. University of Chicago Press, Supplementary Educational Monographs, no. 94, December 1964, pp. 25–33.

86   De Hirsch, Katrina; Jansky, Jeannette J.; and Langford, William S. *Predicting Reading Failure*. New York, Harper & Row, 1966.

86   Bateman, Barbara. "The Efficacy of an Auditory and a Visual Method of First Grade Reading Instruction with Auditory and Visual Learners." *University of Oregon Curriculum Bulletin*, vol. 23, no. 278, May 1967, pp. 6–14.

87   Robinson, Helen M. "Visual and Auditory Modalities Related to Methods for Beginning Reading." *Reading Research Quarterly*, vol. 8, fall 1972, pp. 7–39.

Page
89 Harris, Albert J. "Practical Applications of Reading Research." *Reading Teacher,* March 1976, pp. 559–564.

90 Arter, Judith A., and Jenkins, Joseph R. "Differential Diagnosis—Prescriptive Teaching: A Critical Appraisal." *Review of Educational Research,* vol. 49, no. 4, fall 1979, pp. 517–555.

90 ——. "Examining the Benefits and Prevalence of Modality Considerations in Special Education." *Journal of Special Education,* vol. 11, no. 3, 1977, pp. 281–298.

93 Williams, Joanna. "The ABD's of Reading: A Program for the Learning Disabled." In Resnick and Weaver, eds., *Theory and Practice* . . . (see Chapter 3), vol. 3.

93 Wallach, Michael A. and Lise. "Helping Disadvantaged Children Learn to Read by Teaching Them Phoneme Identification Skills." In Resnick & Weaver, *Theory and Practice* . . . (see Chapter 3), vol. 3.

Chapter 9: "English Isn't Phonetic"

Page
94 Hay, Julie, and Wingo, Charles E. *Reading with Phonics* (teachers' edition), Philadelphia, J. B. Lippincott, 1948.

95 Hanna, Paul R.; Hodges, R. E.; and Hanna, J. S. *Spelling: Structure Strategies.* Boston, Houghton Mifflin, 1971.

95 Bishop, Margaret. *The ABC's and All Their Tricks.* Published by the author, 152–22 Jewel Ave., Flushing, N.Y. 11307, 1978.

96 *The Headway Program. Level B. Foundation. Teacher's Guide.* La Salle, Ill., Open Court, 1979, p. ix.

97 Diehl, Kathryn, and Hodenfield, G. K. *Johnny Still Can't Read—But You Can Teach Him at Home.* Kathryn Diehl, 554 North McDonel, Lima, Ohio 45801, 1979.

98 Foltzer, Monica M., ed. *Professor Phonics Gives Sound Advice.* Manual of Instructions. St. Ursula Academy, 1339 E. McMillan St., Cincinnati, Ohio, 1975.

98 Spalding, Romalda B. and Walter T. *The Writing Road to Reading* (2d ed.). New York, William Morrow & Company, 1969.

99 Barrett, Robert. "Reading War Still Flares" (interview with Kenneth Goodman). *Arizona Republic,* March 30, 1980.

99 Goodman, Yetta M., and Burke, C. S. *Reading Miscue Inventory.* New York, Macmillan, 1972.

Page
99   Jongsma, Eugene A. "The Effect of Training in Miscue Analysis on Teacher's Perceptions of Oral Reading Behaviors." *Reading World,* October 1978, pp. 85–90.

Chapter 10: "Word Calling Isn't Reading"

Page
100   Seashore, Robert H., and Eckerson, I. D. "The Measurement of Individual Differences in General English Vocabularies." *Journal of Educational Psychology,* vol. 31, January 1940, pp. 14–38.

100   Seashore, Robert H. "How Many Words Do Children Know?" *The Packet,* vol. 2, November 1947, pp. 1–7.

100   Seashore, Robert H. "The Importance of Vocabulary in Learning Language Skills." *Elementary English,* vol. 25, no. 14, March 1948, pp. 137–152.

102   Dolch, E. W. "Implications of the Seashore Vocabulary Report." *Elementary English,* 1949, pp. 407–412.

102   Seashore, Robert H., and Seegers, J. C. "How Large Are Children's Vocabularies?" *Elementary English,* vol. 26, no. 4, April 1949, pp. 181–194.

102   Schulman, Mary J., and Havighurst, Robert J. "Relations Between Ability and Social Status in a Midwestern Community. IV: Size of Vocabulary." *Journal of Educational Psychology,* vol. 38, November 1947, pp. 437–442.

102   Colvin, Cynthia M. "A Reexamination of the Vocabulary Question." *Elementary English,* vol. 27, 1951, pp. 350–356.

102   Bryan, Fred E. "How Large Are Children's Vocabularies?" *Elementary School Journal,* December 1952, pp. 10–15.

102   Templin, Mildred C. *Certain Language Skills in Children.* Minneapolis, University of Minnesota Press, 1957.

103   Shibles, Burleigh H. "How Many Words Does a First-Grade Child Know?" *Elementary English,* vol. 31, 1959, pp. 42–47.

103   Chall, *Learning to Read* (see Chapter 3), p. 69 note.

103   Lorge, Irving, and Chall, Jeanne. "Estimating the Size of Vocabularies of Children and Adults: An Analysis of Methodological Issues." *Journal of Experimental Education,* vol. 32, no. 2, winter 1963, pp. 147–157.

Page
105   Carey, Susan. "The Child as Word Learner." In Halle, M.;
       Brennan, J.; and Miller, George A. *Linguistic Theory
       and Psychological Reality.* Cambridge, Mass., MIT
       Press, 1978.
106   Mathews, *Teaching to Read* (see Chapter 2), p. 159.

Chapter 11: "Your Child Isn't Ready"

Page
108   Morphett, Mabel V., and Washburne, Carleton. "When
       Should Children Begin to Read?" *Elementary School
       Journal,* March 1931, pp. 496–503.
110   Ames, Louise Bates. *Is Your Child in the Wrong Grade?*
       New York, Harper & Row, 1966.
110   ——. *Stop School Failure.* New York, Harper & Row, 1972.
110   Ames, Louise Bates, and Chase, Joan Ames. *Don't Push Your
       Preschooler.* New York, Harper & Row, 1974.
111   De Hirsch *et al. Predicting Reading Failure* (see Chapter
       8).
111   MacGinitie, Walter H. "Reading Readiness Research."
       Reading Research Quarterly, spring 1969, vol. 4, no.
       3, pp. 398–410.
112   Durkin, Dolores. "Pre-First Grade Starts in Reading: Where
       Do We Stand?" *Educational Leadership,* December
       1978, pp. 174–177.
112   "Reading and Pre-First-Grade: A Joint Statement of
       Concerns about Present Practices in Pre-First-Grade
       Reading Instruction and Recommendations for Im-
       provement." *Young Children,* vol. 32, no. 6, September
       1977, pp. 25–26.
113   Durkin, Dolores. *Children Who Read Early.* New York,
       Teachers College Press, 1966.
115   Chomsky, Carol. "Write Now, Read Later." In Gazden,
       Courtney B., ed. *Language in Early Childhood Educa-
       tion.* Washington, D.C., National Association for the Ed-
       ucation of Young Children, 1972, pp. 119–126.
115   ——. "Invented Spelling in the Open Classroom." *Word,*
       vol. 27, nos. 1–3, April–December 1971.
115   ——. "Approaching Reading Through Invented Spelling."
       In Resnick and Weaver, *Theory and Practice . . .* (see
       Chapter 3), vol. 2.

Page
116   Montessori, Maria. *The Montessori Method*. New York,
       Schocken Books, 1964, pp. 287 ff.
119   Crain, William C. *Theories of Development*. Englewood
       Cliffs, N.J., Prentice-Hall, 1980, pp. 64–67.
121   Whitehead, Alfred North. *The Aims of Education*. New
       York, Macmillan, 1929, p. 16.

       Chapter 12: "Your Child Is Disabled"

Page
123   Bryant, N. Dale. "Learning Disabilities: A Report on the
       State of the Art." *Teachers College Record*, vol. 75, no.
       3, February 1974, pp. 395–404.
124   "Dyslexia." *The Merck Manual*, 13th ed. Rahway, N.J.,
       Merck & Company, 1977, p. 1061.
126   Orton, Samuel T. *Reading, Writing and Speech Problems
       in Children*. New York, W. W. Norton, 1937.
127   Gillingham, Anna, and Stillman, Bessie W. *Remedial Train-
       ing for Children with Specific Disability in Reading,
       Spelling, and Penmanship*, 7th ed. Cambridge, Mass.,
       Educators Publishing Service, 1960.
128   Slingerland, Beth H. *A Multi-Sensory Approach to Language
       Arts for Specific Language Disability Children*. Cam-
       bridge, Mass., Educators Publishing Service, 1971.
128   Gillingham, Anna. Letter to the editor, *Elementary English*,
       vol. 35, 1958, pp. 119–123.
129   Rawson, Margaret B. "Prognosis in Dyslexia." *Orton Society
       Reprint Series*, no. 13, 1966.
129   Eisenberg, Leon. "Epidemiology of Reading Retardation."
       In Money, John, ed., *The Disabled Reader: Education
       of the Dyslexic Child*. Baltimore, Johns Hopkins Univer-
       sity Press, 1966.
129   Samuels, S. Jay. "Reading Disability?" *Reading Teacher*,
       1970, pp. 270–271, 283.
129   Balow, Bruce. "Perceptual-Motor Activities in the Treat-
       ment of Severe Reading Disability." *Reading Teacher*,
       March 1971, pp. 513–525.
130   Cohen, S. Alan. "Minimal Brain Dysfunction and Practical
       Matters Such as Teaching Kids to Read." *Annals
       of the New York Academy of Sciences*, 1973, pp. 251–
       261.
130   Bryant, "Learning Disabilities" (see above).

Page

130   Bateman, Barbara. "Educational Implications of Minimal Brain Dysfunction." *Reading Teacher*, April 1974, pp. 662–668.

130   Glenn, Hugh W. "The Myth of the Label *Learning Disabled Child.*" *Elementary School Journal*, March 1975, pp. 357–361.

130   Allington, Richard L. "Sticks and Stones . . . But Will Names Never Hurt Them?" *Reading Teacher*, January 1975, pp. 364–369.

130   Pollack, Cecelia. "Neuropsychological Aspects of Reading and Writing." *Orton Society Reprint Series*, no. 73, 1976.

130   Vellutino, Frank R. "Alternative Conceptualizations of Dyslexia; Evidence in Support of a Verbal-Deficit Hypothesis." *Harvard Educational Review*, vol. 17, no. 3, August 1977, pp. 334–353.

131   Kline, "Adolescents with Learning Problems" (see Chapter 5).

131   Penfield, Wilder. *The Mystery of the Mind*. Princeton University Press, 1975.

134   Orton, June L. "The Orton-Gillingham Approach." *Orton Society Reprint Series*, no. 11, 1966.

135   Woodward, Kenneth L. "When Your Child Can't Read." *McCall's*, February 1973.

135   Traub, Nina. *Recipe for Reading*, 2nd ed. Cambridge, Mass., Educators Publishing Service, 1975.

135   Duane, Drake D., and Rome, Paula D. *Developmental Dyslexia*. New York, Insight Publishing Company, 1977.

143   Schweizer, Ilva T. "Orton Revisited." *Reading Teacher*, December 1974, pp. 295–297.

144   Hartman, Nancy C. and Robert K. "Perceptual Handicap or Reading Disability?" *Reading Teacher*, April 1973, pp. 684–695.

144   Delacato, Carl H. *The Treatment and Prevention of Reading Problems*. Springfield, Ill., Carl C. Thomas, 1959.

146   Roswell, Florence G., and Natchez, Gladys. *Reading Disability: A Human Approach to Learning*. (3d ed.) New York, Basic Books, 1977.

146   Osman, Betty B. *Learning Disabilities—A Family Affair*. New York, Random House, 1979.

Chapter 13: "It's the Parents' Fault"

Page
149   Huey, *Psychology and Pedagogy of Reading* (see Chapter 2), pp. 332 ff.

150   Rejai, Mostafa. "On the Failure of Parents in the Educational Process." *Educational Forum*, May 1979, pp. 435–437.

151   Flood, James E. "Parental Styles in Reading Episodes with Young Children." *Reading Teacher*, May 1977, pp. 864–867.

151   Flack, Marjorie. *Ask Mr. Bear.* New York, Macmillan, 1932.

152   Pickering, C. Thomas. *Helping Children Learn to Read.* New York, Chesford, Inc., 1977.

153   Hoskisson, Kenneth; Sherman, Thomas M.; and Smith, Linda L. "Assisted Reading and Parent Involvement." *Reading Teacher*, April 1974, pp. 710–714.

154   Feitelson, Dina. "Chapter 20. Israel." In Downing, John, ed., *Comparative Reading.* New York, Macmillan, 1973.

156   Flesch, *Why Johnny Can't Read* (see Chapter 1).

Chapter 14: "Too Much TV"

Page
157   Torrey, Jane W. "Learning to Read Without a Teacher: A Case Study." *Elementary English*, vol. 46, 1969, pp. 550–556, 658.

158   Durkin, *Children Who Read Early* (see Chapter 11).

161   Thorndike, Robert L. "Causation of Binet IQ Decrements." *Journal of Educational Measurement*, vol. 14, no. 3, fall 1977, pp. 197–202.

162   Diehl, Kathryn. "The Electric Company: Sudden Power Failure." *Associated Press*, August 27, 1976.

Chapter 15: "We Now Teach *All* Children"

Page
163   Jensen, Arthur R. "How Much Can We Boost IQ and Scholastic Achievement?" *Harvard Educational Review*, vol. 39, no. 1, winter 1969, pp. 1–123.

163   Wisler, Burns, and Imamoto, "Follow Through Redux" (see Chapter 4).

Page
163   Hearnshaw, L. S. *Cyril Burt, Psychologist.* Ithaca, N.Y., Cornell University Press, 1979.

163   Guthrie, John T. "Follow Through: A Compensatory Education Experiment." *Reading Teacher,* November 1977, pp. 240–244.

164   Criqui, Orvel A. "An Administrator's View of Reading Programs." *Reading Teacher,* January 1977, pp. 356–358.

164   Hoover, Mary Rhodes. "Characteristics of Black Schools at Grade Level: A Description." *Reading Teacher,* April 1978, pp. 757–762.

166   Doyle, Ann M. "A Grand Ridge Miracle: Its Kids Can Read." West Palm Beach (Fla.) *Post,* March 23, 1980, pp. D1, D5.

167   Durr, William K., and Hickman, Roberta. "Reading Instruction in Soviet Schools: Methods and Materials." *Reading Teacher,* November 1974, pp. 134–140.

Index